STRATEGIC REAL ESTATE INVESTING

Harrison
WEALTH
Shippensburg, PA

STRATEGIC REAL ESTATE INVESTING

CREATING PASSIVE
INCOME THROUGH
REAL ESTATE MASTERY

BILLY EPPERHART

Published by Harrison House Publishers
Shippensburg, PA 17257

Cover design by: Eileen Rockwell.

ISBN 13 TP: 978-1-6803-1479-3

ISBN 13 eBook: 978-1-6803-1480-9

ISBN 13 HC: 978-1-6803-1482-3

ISBN 13 LP: 978-1-6803-1481-6

For Worldwide Distribution, Printed in the U.S.A.

1 2 3 4 5 6 7 8 / 25 24 23 22 21

CONTENTS

Foreword. 7

Introduction. 9

Part One 15

Chapter 1:
Triple X Factor: A 30,000-foot View of How to Build Wealth. 17

Chapter 2:
Developing Real Estate Income 29

Part Two 45

Chapter 3:
Why I Like Real Estate. 47

Chapter 4:
How to Identify the Best Markets to Buy. 59

Chapter 5:
Keys to Finding Bargain Properties 65

Chapter 6:

    14 Mistakes Investors Make 79

Chapter 7:

    Top 10 Secrets of Real Estate Financing. 103

Part Three. 127

Chapter 8:

    Section 8 Housing. 129

Chapter 9:

    How to Profit Big Buying Vacation Properties 139

Part Four. 163

Chapter 10:

    How to Inspect a Property 165

Chapter 11:

    Legal Matters in Real Estate. 173

Part Five 185

Chapter 12:

    Fixing and Flipping 187

    Glossary. 207

    Appendix. 217

    About the Author 233

FOREWORD

If you are reading this book, chances are you either want to be a real estate investor, or you already are one who wants to get some powerful "nuggets" that can make your path to real estate success both faster and easier. Real estate investing, like any business, has a learning curve. It has been said that it takes 10,000 hours or so to become a master at any profession, and real estate is no exception. Thus, if you tried to figure it out by trial and error for 10 hours per week, it would take you approximately 19 years to master real estate investing. You can, however, cut that learning curve significantly by leveraging other people's experience. However, if you do so, make sure that you leverage the experience of someone who is already a master at his trade. Billy Epperhart is undeniably such a person.

I was quite honored and humbled when Billy asked me to write the foreword for this book. I have known Billy in a personal and professional manner for many years and can testify that Billy is a savvy, experienced, professional, and most of all, ethical real estate investor. He is also very generous with his time and knowledge to help others. There are so many false prophets promising fast profits that it can be hard to discern who is for real and who is not. Well, I can unequivocally say that Billy Epperhart is the REAL deal!

I have been a practicing attorney and real estate investor myself for 30 years and have authored six books on real estate, so I know how much work goes into writing one. Billy is already a wealthy man through his own real estate investment, so he doesn't need to sell books for income. But I know that Billy is a man who believes that if God gives you the opportunity to be successful at something, you have the responsibility to teach others how to follow in your footsteps.

Not every experienced real estate investor can convey the principles of profitable investing in a way that a reader can follow; Billy does it in a succinct way that makes it easy for the reader to understand. And, just as importantly, Billy inspires the reader to want to take action and be a successful investor.

Aside from the financial rewards, I have received tremendous personal pleasure from working with Billy throughout the years. Though, you may not get the opportunity to work with him personally as I did, you now have a wonderful alternative—to learn and use the knowledge contained in this book.

Read it twice, and more importantly, put his principles to work. You and your family will be immensely grateful!

Bill Bronchick
Real estate attorney, coach, investor
Author of six real estate books

INTRODUCTION

You may have picked up this book for several reasons. You may be a beginning wealth-builder looking for ways to increase your income or build your net worth. You may be tired of the ups and downs of the stock market and looking for a more consistent return on your money. Yet, more than likely, you picked up this book because you want to be financially free. Whatever your reasons, I believe this book will empower you to take the first steps and beyond toward building wealth and walking the road to financial success.

Meanwhile, let me tell you about a defining moment in my life that motivated me to build wealth and reach for success. I also share this story in my book *Money Mastery*. In fact, I often share this story because it changed my life so dramatically.

As a much younger man, I was head of an organization that hosted a major conference. By major, I mean there were several private jets parked on the runway. We had some heavy hitters in the house! These guest speakers flew in on private jets that their organizations owned.

When the conference was over, two of the guys who flew in on their own planes joined me in the mountains for a couple of days of rest and relaxation. We went to a huge hot springs pool in the mountains of Colorado. As we stood in the heated water that was a little less than waist deep, one of the guys looked at me and said, "Billy, what kind of plans have you made for retirement?"

Usually, a conversation like this would start with, "So, did you enjoy the drive up?" or "What did you think about the conference?" But this guy just jumped right in and asked me what kind of plans I had for retirement. I thought about my small real estate investments and what little money I had put aside, but before I could respond, he said something that shook me to my core. He said, "If I did not have my job, I would be 'broke' in 90 days. I would literally be out on the street."

That terrified me! At the time, I was aspiring to be one of these men who had flown in on their organization's jets. That was my goal! I had a little bit of investment in real estate and had saved a little money, but I was mostly focusing on growing and building my career. So, when he said that, it was one of those "aha moments" for me.

When I returned home from the rest and relaxation trip, I was a man on a mission. I was determined to replace all my salary and benefits with passive income—income I didn't have to work for. At the time, my salary, benefits, and travel felt like a pretty big paycheck, so that was a significant goal for me to try to reach. But I was determined, so I set my face like a flint, and here's what happened.

I caught the real estate market at just the right time in the United States. During this time, I was developing and practicing the formulas that I now teach in my Real Estate Mastery course. I was learning how not to overpay for real estate. After the first ten properties, and over the course of two and a half years, I finally reached my goal of replacing my income with passive income. I didn't have to sell something or put in X number of hours to collect this extra income.

I remember the specific day I replaced my salary and benefits with passive income. It was a monumental moment for me! I was sitting in the parking lot in front of a Starbucks, enjoying a Quad Grande Americano—no cream, no sugar. It's what I call a "man's man's drink." As I was sitting there, I received a call from one of my property managers and my accountant. In those days, as I began to grow and expand, I had multiple property managers and one accountant.

This particular manager was handling a lot of property at the time and told me I had reached my goal—I had replaced all of my income with passive income. Suddenly I felt so *free*, and on that day, I truly became the master of my money! I know you also want that kind of freedom, which is why I'm sharing what I've learned to help you get there.

An Orchard versus a Garden

While my primary residence has been in Colorado for over 30 years, I am originally from the Houston, Texas, area. Houston is a hot humid area with lots of mosquitos, roaches, and pecan trees.

Mosquitos and roaches are things to avoid, but pecans are good for baking and delicious for just eating plain.

As a boy, my friends and I would pick up pecans that had fallen to the ground and place them in burlap sacks. After we had collected about 20 pounds, we would take them to the feed store and sell them to the store for so much per pound. It was a great way to earn some extra money. For years we would pick up pecans that had fallen to the ground from the same trees. In fact, some years we threw wooden sticks up into the branches to make more pecans fall out, which in turn, made us more money.

It never occurred to me as a kid that actually owning pecan trees would be a good strategy for producing a whole lot more income until I met my wife's grandparents who owned a pecan orchard. They had several different varieties of pecans—some were sold for much higher per pound than the native pecans my friends and I had collected. At harvest time, large tarps would be placed under the trees, and the trees were shaken until the tarps were covered with pecans.

Because my wife's grandparents owned an orchard, they were much more intentional about producing higher quality pecans. Their harvest methods were much quicker, and they made a lot more money.

The same grandparents also grew a large garden every year. They would annually till the soil to make it ready for planting then plant the seeds again. It would take several months for the newly planted seeds to grow into a plant that was healthy enough to produce vegetables. I always loved the fresh tomatoes and cucumbers that were harvested.

There was a pronounced amount of effort required to plant, weed, and harvest the vegetables, and it had to be done all over again and again every year. On the other hand, the pecan orchard did not have to be replanted every year. Some years the trees had to be sprayed for worms, and at times, there was the need to do some "grafting" to develop a new variety of pecan. But overall, the orchard required much less work than the garden. In fact, it has been years since they both passed away, and those same pecan trees are producing abundantly even today. It's like they are programed to automatically yield a harvest every year.

Why are orchards and gardens important to you and me? The "secret sauce" to building wealth is to develop an orchard—not just a garden.

The garden is more like a job while owning an orchard that produces fruit year after year is like owning real estate that produces rental income. You still have to manage the orchard and "spray" for worms from time to time, but the trees keep generating fruit without a lot of effort. In fact, the Internal Revenue Service (IRS) calls someone who spends 750 hours per year on acquiring, rehabbing, and owning real estate a full-time real estate professional. That's about 15 hours a week as opposed to 40 hours a week that a regular job requires.

The truth is, once proper systems are created and the right property managers are in place, you will be able to spend many fewer than 15 hours per week in real estate. In the first chapter of this book, I will describe in detail what it means to position yourself to live off your passive income (rental income) instead of earned income (job income).

You are also welcome to visit our website, wealthbuilders.org, which contains an abundance of free information you can access through our blogs and vlogs on the subjects of wealth building, real estate, entrepreneurship, and investing.

Much success to you in your wealth-building journey!

Billy Epperhart

PART ONE

CHAPTER 1

TRIPLE X FACTOR: A 30,000-FOOT VIEW OF HOW TO BUILD WEALTH

Whenever I would hear different teachings on wealth building, it felt like I was standing too close to an elephant. For instance, if a man did not know what an elephant was, and someone asked him the question, "What is an elephant?" he might be stumped to answer. If he only saw the trunk of the elephant, he might say, "Oh, an elephant is a hose." Or, perhaps, if he looked up and only saw the side of the elephant, he might say, "Oh, an elephant is a wall." Or, if he only saw the tail, he might say, "An elephant is a rope." In other words, the man associated the whole object with only one part. But the truth is, an elephant is more than a trunk, a side, or a tail. An elephant is all those things.

In the same way, I struggled for a long time to fit all the different lessons on wealth building into one solid idea. I was looking for wealth building in simple terms. If I learned something that was about debt freedom, I'd put it over in the debt-freedom compartment in my brain. But I knew that building wealth was more than eliminating debt. I knew the trunk was attached to an elephant, so what I was really dealing with was an elephant.

Finally, after many years of experience, discussion, and learning, I received the Triple X Factor. This gave me the true 30,000-foot view of wealth building. I finally saw the whole elephant or the whole picture all at once.

Triple X Factor

Understanding this concept on wealth building can position you from being mastered by money to the point of mastering money. I call it the *Triple X Factor*.

There are three levels within the Triple X Factor—First X, Second X, and Third X. First X Income is the starting point when you work and get paid for that work. Second X Income is a place of great freedom because you have and manage assets that pay you. Third X is a place of philanthropy and making a difference in other people's lives. At the Third X, you're donating or investing the majority of your income or assets for the benefit of others.

To begin wealth building, you must first find out where you are financially. A safe guess at the average American household income is about $50,000. For some states it is higher and for some it is lower, but this is a good starting point for our illustration.

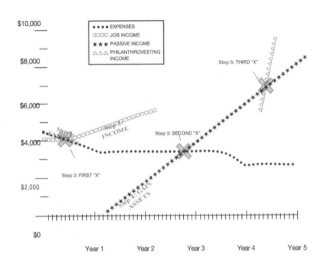

When you look at the indebtedness of a typical household in the U.S., you will see more money going out every month than coming in. If $50,000 represents the average annual income in the U.S., then $54,000 represents the average annual household expenses. So, we are left with one question: How can someone spend more per year than they actually make?

Unique to western nations is the phenomenon of consumer credit. We can easily buy things that immediately depreciate in value by using consumer credit. We can buy things like TVs and clothes on credit because we have credit cards or other types of installment accounts. Therefore, in America, it is exceptionally easy to spend more than you make.

Each dot represents one month of expenses. So, for this illustration, at the beginning, we have about $4,500 going out each month. It's important to position yourself in order to build wealth. I recommend building your own personal chart based off this.

1. Plot your expenses each month.

To fill out your own chart, you need to be very honest about your expenses. Start with the month you're in right now. Begin to chart your monthly expenses. For instance, let's say you start in April, and the total outgo of expenses in March was $2,500. You would place an asterisk at the $2,500 mark. Then at the end of April, you would place an asterisk representing how much you spent in April.

Once you start implementing the tools in this book, you should begin to see your expenses go down. This will allow you to start paying off your debt while learning how to handle your finances better. However, for a lot of people, expenses don't come down. They remain the same or may even go up until they can get control of their spending. If this happens to you, that's okay. Start where you are, and with time, prayer, and work, you will eventually learn how to master this expense line.

2. Plot your income each month.

Each square in the line represents monthly income. Chart your first month's income in the same way that you charted your first monthly expenses. This line will probably stay horizontal for a while. But again, after you implement what you learn in this book, you'll be able to start bringing value to the marketplace. And when you start bringing value to the marketplace, your income will begin to go up.

3. Build your First X.

Now for some people, the First X is in good shape. In other words, they have more income than expenses. If this is the case, they can start building the Second X. But for most people, the First X is going to be in rougher shape. This means that they have more expenses than income. In this instance, the squares representing monthly income will stay even for now, but the dots—monthly expenses—are going to come down.

Most people will be able to start controlling their expenses, especially their consumer debt, before they start increasing their income. That's completely normal. Start working on your expenses immediately by cutting things out, making extra, or driving down debt. It will take a little longer to grow your income.

When it comes to your income, always remember this: You take value to the marketplace not time. Most people think they take time because they get paid per hour, but the truth is, money is attracted not pursued. So, when you start working on yourself harder than you do on your job, you will get paid more for your job. This is because you become more valuable.

As your expenses begin to come down and your income begins to go up, you start to form the First X. In other words, you are in a position to begin building wealth. The First X is a great place to be. You either get out of debt, or gain control of it, and start mastering your finances. There is some teaching available out there on this aspect, but there's not a lot on how to reach the Second X.

4. Gain assets.

Keep graphing your income and expense lines every month so you can monitor exactly where you are. For example, as the First X forms, you'll notice a gap developing between the line of squares and the dots. That gap is the excess capital that you now have available to you. What you do with that excess capital determines whether or not you will build wealth. You might be tempted to just spend it all, thereby not building any wealth. The good news is that at least you're not getting into more consumer debt by doing this (hopefully), but the bad news is that you are still not building wealth.

The real key to building wealth is learning to invest your excess capital. Put that excess capital to work so you can begin to gain assets that produce income in your life. Start using this gap to create Second X income. For some people, it may take two, three, or even four years to reach a point where they have any excess capital to deploy or invest. That's okay. Stay with it, and you'll get there!

In this particular example, we're looking at a 12-month period. Pay attention to the first asterisk on the left. That asterisk represents your first investment. You probably won't have enough money to put a down payment on a piece of real estate, but you will have enough to open a savings account.

Several years ago, I was teaching at a conference at the Omni Hotel in Dallas, Texas. When I finished teaching on real estate, two huge guys, each about 6'5", came up to me and said, "We're ready to invest in real estate!"

They were pumped up from the talk, so I looked at them and said, "Well, do you have any money?"

"Well, no, we don't have any money," they said. "But we're excited and ready to invest."

Here's how I answered them: "When you have $10,000 in your possession, call me. I'll fly to Dallas at my expense, and I'll teach you how to buy your first investment property."

Six months later, one of the guys called me. He had $10,000, so I flew to Texas and helped him get started. Today he owns more than 60 individual properties—multi-family units and single-family houses.

You might ask, "What does this have to do with the first asterisk?"

Actually, it provides a lot of insight. Let me explain. This young man returned home and immediately started saving. He had a good income and put some money into a savings account. That was his first asterisk that began to build his income line to reach the Second X. By doing this, he positioned himself to begin acquiring assets. The goal is that the asterisks, representing income from assets, will progress upward and form a line.

Of course, if you put your money in a savings account, your return will be very low. That's not a lot of income. Instead, if you put your money into assets with a better return, the asterisks will really start to accelerate.

A simple illustration of an asset that brings income is rental properties (single-family) with positive cash flow. The more investments of this type you can accumulate, the more the snowball will start rolling in the right direction.

As you build wealth, all the sudden, your cars and mortgage will be paid off. The beauty of this is that when your house and cars are paid off, it doesn't cost a lot to live. The dots, or your expenses, will continue to come down.

Note: You can start the asterisks without ever accomplishing the First X. If you're not in a financial position to acquire assets, you can create assets instead and start the asterisks early. An example of creating an asset is starting a business outside of your day job, like an eBay or Etsy shop, that has immediate cash flow. Then you can use that cash flow from the business to start investing in assets or paying off debt.

Another way to do this would be to borrow for the purpose of investing in assets. I know many people who have started investing in real estate by taking out a second mortgage on their personal home. If they have enough real estate knowledge and acquire assets slowly (at least in the beginning), they can build Second X income from that acquired real estate.

5. Build the Second X.

The key to the Triple X Factor is when the asterisks begin to take off as you acquire excess capital and put it into things that produce income for you. You will start investing and receiving better and better returns.

Here's what happens once this occurs: The dots will continue to go down, and all the sudden, the asterisks will cross the dots.

This means that your cost of living is covered by passive income. The moment that the asterisks become more than your cost of living is the moment you become financially free. That's the moment when, if you want, you can quit your job.

I was able to reach financial independence in my personal life in two and a half years. But for some people, it may take a lot longer than that. It could take some people ten years to do this.

A lot of people ask me what their first goal should be when starting to build wealth. I always tell them what the Triple X Factor says: Your first goal—your first big goal—should be to replace your earned income with passive income. That's it! That is the key to start experiencing financial independence.

In our seminars, we teach that there are six primary categories of passive income. Please note there are more, but these six will help you focus on the right types of income.

- RENT FROM REAL ESTATE
- CAPITAL DISTRIBUTIONS FROM A BUSINESS
- DIVIDENDS FROM STOCK
- INTEREST FROM BONDS AND CDs
- ROYALITIES FROM OIL AND GAS
- ROYALITIES FROM SONGS AND BOOKS

If you notice, this income is not about buying and selling anything. For example, learning to buy and flip real estate is an effective money-making strategy but the income from it is not considered passive income. It is considered earned income and taxed at an increased level. If fact, we do cover flipping in our workshops, but the focus of this book is to teach you how to build passive income through real estate. We teach how to buy and sell (flip) real estate as an income strategy because most investors need to find more capital for down payments and repair costs in order to continue to build their real estate portfolio.

The financial industry in America tells you to put your asterisk money (see Triple X chart) in a 401(k), an individual retirement account (IRA), or some other type of retirement account. It's definitely wise to have a retirement account set up—but that is a slow process. It can take a long time to build up wealth that way!

Many people who retire with a decent portfolio have never taken the time to learn how to invest because they never understood how taxes could steal their wealth. When they retire, they end up paying more taxes in what we call *tax-deferred accounts* than they were paying when they were actually working and earning a salary. The minute they start pulling that money out of those normal IRAs and 401(k) plans, they have to pay earned-income tax on that money. After all is said and done, they end up having much less than they thought they had.

The good news is that we have another instrument called the *Roth IRA.* Young people should certainly take advantage of this tool because that money grows tax-free down the road. Then when you pull the money out, you don't have to pay earned-income tax on it. The best news, however, is that when you reach this point of financial independence, you can continue to grow an amazing portfolio, invest in all kinds of things, and truly begin to build wealth.

6. Build the Third X.

Remember on the First X when the dotted line crossed the line of squares, and we had a gap? The same thing happens here. When the asterisks cross the dotted line, we will have another gap that represents excess capital again. It's at that point that I marked: "Quit job!"

You may ask, "What do you do with that new excess capital?" This is the moment you can choose to really begin building wealth. This is where the Third X comes in.

Somewhere in that excess capital gap, you will reach a point where you can start giving all your excess income away and invest your assets for social impact and making a difference. Now everything you earn—100% from this passive income above the point where the asterisks meets the triangles—is surplus! You have reached the place where you and your family are already taken care of. You're financially independent. You could even quit your job if you chose to do so. You are completely and totally financially free!

CHAPTER 2

DEVELOPING REAL ESTATE INCOME

Another way to think about wealth building that aligns with the concept of the Triple X factor is what I call the *Three Levels of Money*. Robert Kiyosaki in his series of *Rich Dad* books insightfully outlines these concepts.

LEVEL 1

Money that you
WORK FOR
Purpose:
-Tithe/Offering
-Asset Building
-Live Out of
Type:
-Job
Category:
-Employee
-Self Employed
-Non-leveraged income

LEVEL 2

Money that
WORKS FOR YOU
Purpose:
-Tithe/Offering
-Foundational Wealth
-Asset Building
Type:
-Asset Income
Category:
-Business Owner
-Investor

LEVEL 3

Money that
WORKS WITHOUT YOU
Purpose
-Philanthrophy
-Kingdom Investing
-Multiple Assets
-Preserving Wealth
-Growing Wealth
-City/Nation Transformation
Type:
-Absentee Asset Income
Category:
-Investor

This chart shows three levels of income: Level 1, money you work for; Level 2, money that works for you; and Level 3, money that works without you. In this manual, I will teach you how to reach Level 2 income through real estate. These three levels of income match perfectly with the three Xs. The first X matches level one. The second X matches level two and so on.

Baby Boomers and the Stock Market

Twenty-two percent of America's population is composed of baby boomers who will soon begin retiring, and therefore, withdraw money from the stock market. Imagine the impact that will have when the only way they know how to get the money they need to live off of is what they work for. They will have to sell the stocks that are in the market. So what will happen to the stock market when 22% per cent of the population begins to take out money? We've got some challenges facing America in the next 10-25 years and people must become financially educated. It's important that they learn how to make money and live off of the assets they have acquired.

Another way to look at the stock market versus real estate is to know that the stock market at the time of this writing had a value of 30 trillion dollars and single-family real estate had a value of 33 trillion dollars. However, there are 60 million people who are investing in the 30 trillion-dollar U.S. stock market and approximately only 1 million investors who are investing in the 33 trillion-dollar single family market. That means that the pie is much smaller investing in the stock market. And in the stock market somebody has to lose in order for someone else to win. Yet, real estate has the capacity to be a win-win for everyone.

Also, many retired folks today will tell you the greatest challenge they face is not just getting the money they need to live off of but how to take the assets they have and produce an income stream that is sufficient enough after they pay their taxes. Retirement accounts that are held in traditional 401(k) plans and IRA plans are taxed at earned income rates which can be well over 30%. So, if your income from retirement accounts is $100,000 in gross income, it is possible you would have to pay $30,000 or more in income taxes. With real estate, it is possible to receive $100,000 in income and pay zero in taxes. I will discuss that later in the book.

The challenge is that we know how to earn and save, but we don't know how to invest or make money with assets to live off of. That is what I will be teaching you in the following chapter and throughout the rest of this book.

Step One: Understand What You Want

The first thing you need to do is to decide what level of income you want to receive without working. Let's break up some of the categories: $25,000 or less is living at the poverty level. From $25,000-$50,000 would be lower-middle class. From $50,000-$100,000 would be middle class. $100,000-$150,000 and up would be in the upper-middle class. $150,000+ would be in the affluent range. $1,000,000+ would be what we call upper class. The first step is to decide where you want to be, which will determine how much money you need to make from your assets.

We all want different things when it comes to our desires, goals, and dreams. I heard one man say, "I need $250,000 a year just to do everything that I want to do with my family." That's a pretty big statement. So, then what does it take? What do you have to learn? What assets do you need to acquire to receive $250,000 in income without working every year? The choice is a personal one.

Step Two: Understand Your Net Worth

The second step in developing Second X income is to understand how net worth affects your income. Net worth, in its simplest definition, is assets minus liabilities. Assets are stocks and bonds, real estate, businesses that you own, or any other property of value. For most people, liabilities are consumer debt, credit cards, installment loans, and any money that you may owe against your real estate or some of your assets. If you take the assets minus the liabilities, that tells you what your net worth is right now.

A lot of people ask me how to find what their net worth should be. I've got a simple formula for you: First, multiply your age by your income. Let's say you're 40 years old, and your income is $50,000 a year. Multiply your age times your income, or in other words, 40 x $50,000 a year. That's $2,000,000. Then divide that by 10. You come up with $200,000, which is the net worth range for a 40-year-old with $50,000 in income a year.

(AGE x INCOME) / 10 = NET WORTH

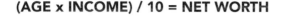

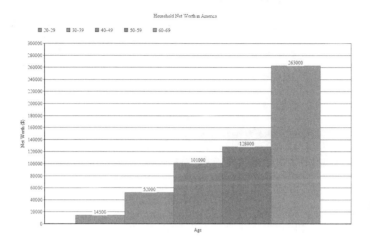

To give you help on an age chart, this is what the age of household net worth is in America today. In these age ranges, 20-29 is $14,500; 30-39 is $52,000; 40-49 is $101,000; 50-59 is $128,000; and 60-64 is $263,000

Your net worth represents your assets minus your liabilities. The question is, how much can you earn from your net worth? I will give you a pretty conservative statement here just to give you some boundaries. When we get into more real estate investing, you'll see that you can actually withdraw more than this.

Right now, without over-risking, you can withdraw about 4-5% out of your net worth annually. Even in the 60-64 age category we gave you, which is typically people who are retired or getting ready to retire and generally only have $263,000 in net worth. This means they can withdraw about $13,150 per year. Most people can't live off of that amount, so they need other sources of income like Social Security or pensions.

Now that you understand you can withdraw 4-5% of your net worth per year, you have a good starting place for what your goals should be and where you need to be.

Step Three: Increase Your Net Worth

Since net worth has such an important part to play in developing Second X income, the third step in developing this income is increasing your net worth. One way to increase your net worth is to aggressively acquire assets. You should begin to look at different returns in the categories of businesses, real estate, stocks, and bonds.

The second way to increase your net worth is to eliminate consumer debt. Most people don't realize how much interest they pay on their credit cards. All that money that you're paying to another company in interest rates is increasing their balance sheet. You're helping their net worth, but you're literally giving away money.

You should place a priority on eliminating consumer debt.

There is debt you can utilize to be able to develop Level 2 income. For example, when you borrow money for real estate or money to buy businesses, you begin to control assets that produce income. Most people won't hesitate to put a plasma television on their credit card, which is consumer debt. Yet, if we told them to come up with $10,000 and invest it in an asset, they get really uncomfortable. That shows you how warped our thinking is. Plasma televisions won't make you any money, but real estate, stocks, and businesses will.

Step Four: Keep a Financial Statement

The fourth step is to keep an updated financial statement. It doesn't have to be really technical. All you need to do is put what your assets are worth on one side, what your liabilities are, how much you owe, and include all the payments. Don't just record the monthly payments. When you're looking at your financial statement, you want to look at the total amount you owe in your liabilities. Then subtract that from the value of your assets, which gives you your net worth. I have included a sample financial statement in the Appendix of this book.

Every time something changes—for example, your liability is increased—write it down. If your credit card bill goes up, put that on there. If you have a particular asset that goes up or the return is magnified and it's worth more, put that on there. Keep an updated financial statement to know where you are in the game.

Step Five: Focus on Return

The fifth thing that you need to do is to focus on return. Many people have said that the greatest invention has been compound interest. When you focus on return, what you're looking at is literally cash on cash return. In other words, how can you take $10,000 and get a 6%, 12%, 20%, or 100% return?

There is a rule that says if you divide 72 by an interest rate, the resulting number is the number of years it would take your money to double at that rate. For example, if you were able to take $10,000 and get a 24% interest rate return, your money would double in three years. If you were able to get a 20% return, your money would double in 3.6 years. If you were able to get a 15% return, your money would double in 4.8 years. We go all the way down. If you were able to get 12% return, your money would double in six years. At 6%, return, of course, the rule of 72, shows your money would double in 12 years.

Interest Rate	Years to Double
1%	72
2%	36
3%	24
4%	18
5%	14
6%	12
7%	10.3
8%	9
9%	8
10%	7.2
11%	6.5
12%	6
13%	5.5
14%	5.1
15%	4.8

It's not overly difficult to get 100%, cash-on-cash return on real estate because of leverage. It's important to focus on the return so you know which assets are valuable to invest in.

Step Six: Become Income Oriented

The sixth step is to become income oriented. For example, many years ago, stocks paid pretty good dividends. Some people were able to live full-time out of their dividends. Around the 1950s or so that began to change and, today the only way someone can actually make money off of stocks is selling it. The dividends just aren't high enough to earn an income anymore.

In real estate, you don't have to sell anything to generate income because you can rent the property. As one author has so appropriately described it, it's the difference between killing a cow to eat and milking a cow repeatedly. We're looking to produce an income stream or cash flow that we can live out of and become financially independent.

In order to become income oriented, you want to generate income without selling your asset. Your goal, when we talk about being income oriented, is to replace your employment income. In other words, you don't have to work in order to be paid, but you do have to manage your assets. This gives you more time to work on building an income stream and building wealth in your life. You need to develop assets that bring enough income in to replace your employment income.

Step Seven: Accelerate Your Capital

Then, the next major step you need to take is to accelerate your capital. I have a lesson that I like to teach called "The $10,000 Real Estate Millionaire." The idea is that you take a specific pot of money, and you accelerate it so you control more and more assets that, in turn, will appreciate and produce more and more income. So, the same $10,000 down payment on a $100,000 house can be utilized over and over to acquire an unlimited amount of houses. You buy the first house with the $10,000 down payment, and then sometime later you refinance that house and take the $10,000 back out and use it to buy another $100,000 house. You now have two $100,000 houses that have been acquired with the same $10,000. Just refinance and repeat until you have acquired the number of properties to reach your goal.

Dormant home equity is the most common place where people do not accelerate their capital. It is one of the most common places that assets stay tied up. I'm not an advocate of leveraging all the way up to your eyeballs so that you can't pay your bills, and you shouldn't take money out of your homes to buy things that go down in value. In other words, don't use your home equity to buy things that most people use consumer debt for.

I advocate that you use your home equity to acquire more assets that increase in value. You can borrow up to 90% as long as you're able to make the payment and maintain a positive of at least $300 per month.

Another way you can accelerate your capital is to purchase one home a year with the same $10,000. Instead of taking $100,000 you just take $10,000. You buy a $100,000 house and then you refinance. You do what's called a *cash out refi* on that property, and you get your $10,000 back in 12 months. You use that $10,000 to buy another house. You continue to invest the original $10,000 over 10 years, and you acquire 10 homes.

In order to do this successfully, your knowledge has to increase. You have to understand the risks that are involved and what your downsides could be.

Another example is to utilize $100,000 in home equity that would enable you buy ten $100,000 homes in one year by placing 10% down, which is $10,000 on each one. You now have $1,000,000 in assets plus your home. In other words, what you control and the ability of your assets to increase has now become tenfold because you aren't leaving it in one place, but you're accelerating it.

What is 5% appreciation increase in just one year on these new properties? For example, you've now acquired $1,000,000 in assets over and above what you had with the $100,000.

Just a 5% appreciation increase on these properties is $50,000 in one year. In other words, just the appreciation has made you $50,000 back on the $100,000 you put in.

Step Eight: Invest with a Formula

In buying and holding real estate, one simple formula that I use is your total investment—that includes all of your repair costs, acquisition carrying costs—should be no more than 80% of the real value of the property. Then, you want a $300 a month positive cash flow after principal, interest, taxes, insurance, and management.

Most people will say yes to anything when it comes to investing. But you cannot say yes to everything or you will get burned. You've got to learn to say no to certain things, and when you invest with a formula, you will know which opportunities are good opportunities for you.

Again, you want no more than 80% total investment in the property, and you want a $300 a month in positive cash flow. That protects you on the cash flow side, and it also protects you on the actual value side.

Step Nine: Be a Resilient Learner

Another key to developing Second X income is to become a resilient learner. Whether you are a business owner or a real estate investor, you must learn to become a problem solver.

Several years ago, I received a water bill for about $500 a month over a period of two months. It was a duplex, and back then it had one water meter running for both units. This particular property had such potential for a strong cash flow, but I got so discouraged. Then, finally, somebody came to me and asked why I didn't put in dual water meters. We began to look around, and we found someone who was willing to work with the city and give us a really good deal. The problem was completely solved, and the tenants became responsible for their own water bill. This tremendously increased my bottom line. I learned a very important lesson that day that I never forgot. Make sure there are water meters for each unit!

There are five things you need to put into practice in order to be a resilient learner.

Learn from your mistakes. In other words, you will never learn to build businesses, invest in real estate, or learn how to work with stocks unless you're willing to learn from your mistakes and become a resilient learner. Anyone who is going to be an investor moving up to the Second X income has got to be willing to learn from mistakes.

Learn to get in the game. If I were teaching the game of baseball, I could stand on the side all day and instruct players with video, but no one would ever really learn until they got on the field and in the game. Real coaching doesn't take place in a vacuum on the sidelines. Real coaching takes place in the middle of the game.

For example, if I explained to you that properties you buy—especially multi-units—need to have separate metering, you would understand conceptually. But you wouldn't understand the urgency of getting that right until you had to pay the bills. So, when it comes to moving to Second X income, you've got to be willing to get into the game of investing and business ownership in order to be able to learn how to make money.

Learn to develop a team. Have people that know more than you do on your team. In the real estate business, you want bankers, mortgage brokers, a good real estate agent, a good property manager, and good contractors. Developing a team will allow you to have the kind of income that you need.

Learn historical returns. If you look at historical returns across the board, you'll see that U.S. small-cap stocks have been 12%, U.S. large-cap stocks have been 10%, foreign stocks have returned 10%, U.S. real estate is 10%, U.S. oil and gas has been 8%, corporate bonds are 7%, foreign bonds 7%, treasury bonds 6%, money markets and CDs 4%, treasury bills 3%, and gold returns 3%. It's imperative that you understand the historical returns on what you're planning to put your money in because that will inform the potential return on those assets right now.

Learn to rely on systems. You've got to have a team of different players that help you become successful because you can't do everything by yourself. This breeds the system. The formula we just described, the team you use, and the documentation and policies you use all become a part of the system. Having systems makes decision-making easier because good systems anticipate problems ahead of time.

For example, let's say tenants damage a property. A good system in place in advance will make this easier for you to handle. Before a tenant even moves in, you need to outline what repair costs could be needed and how they would be charged, billed, and collected. Also, systems make sure that everyone on your team, your customers, and your tenants are clear on your expectations.

Some people believe that in order to be rich, you have to be born rich. This is far from true, and I hope my book will teach you that you can build your own wealth. Investing in real estate is hard when you first get started, I won't sugarcoat it. But as you learn, you will get better and the various components will become second nature. In the next chapter, I will discuss why I believe real estate is worth the investment of your time and your money.

PART TWO

CHAPTER 3

WHY I LIKE REAL ESTATE

There are many different types of investments, but I am convinced after several years of reviewing investments and investing myself, that real estate is definitely the best. Below I have listed the reasons that I like real estate as an investment.

Demand

The first reason is the built-in demand for real estate. Everybody needs a place to live. In most other businesses, you have to market your product in order to get it in front of the customer and sell it. In real estate, the demand for a place to live is consistent and high. Sometimes you have to advertise a property for rent, but people are inherently looking for a place to live.

Leverage

The next reason why I like real estate is leverage. If you have $10,000 in the stock market, it would buy $10,000 in stock, giving you $10,000 in stock assets. If you received a 10% return that year on those stocks, it would be $1,000.

However, because of leverage in real estate, you're able to take that same $10,000 to actually purchase a $100,000 property. The 10% return is not on the $10,000 you put in but on the $100,000 asset that you acquired with the $10,000. So your return is $10,000. It's literally 100% cash-on-cash return.

Any time you're using leverage, it can work both ways. In other words, leverage not only can magnify your returns, but it can also magnify your losses. There have only been two times real estate has depreciated in America and that was during the Great Depression and the Great Recession. In some areas, it went down by almost half but within five years it was back to it previous levels or even higher. Outside of those two major events, historically residential real estate has increased by about 6% a year.

Because of this historical increase, leverage is a powerful thing. You're able to magnify your returns and tremendously increase the return on your cash because of the power of leverage. You're able to take a little bit of money and control a much larger asset. That's one of the keys to understanding how to build wealth. When you're starting from nothing to build wealth, leverage gives you such a tremendous advantage on being able to magnify your returns on investment.

Cash Flow

Another reason I like real estate investing is the cash flow. Remember, wealth is an income stream. When you buy and hold property, a tenant actually pays for your asset. You collect rent from them, and while your asset is going up in value every year, someone else is paying for it.

What if I could show you a formula where you could purchase 30 homes and make a positive cash flow of $300 a month off those 30 homes? You could end up making $100,000 a year, tax-free for the rest of your life. It's really pretty simple to understand. You purchase 30 homes, say, over three years' time that have a cash flow of $300 per house per month. That's $300 times 30 houses which is $9000 per month times 12 months equaling $108,000 per year. By the time you reach 30 houses, you will have a favorable classification from the IRS that allows the income to be tax deferred or tax-free to you. That favorable classification from the IRS considers you a full-time real estate professional, which can offer you definite benefits. I explain below in the section called "Tax Benefits."

It's tax-free because of depreciation, which means you have the opportunity to depreciate those properties on a 1/27th scale. When you look at it, you get about $3,700 a year per house as a deduction from your taxes because of depreciation. That depreciation covers the profits you show on your house. Basically, you show no positive income off a property because of depreciation, and you're able to shelter your income so it's tax-free. For all the accountants reading this it is technically tax deferred, but to you as the investor it will greatly reduce the taxes you owe.

Then, when you are getting ready to sell it, you actually can roll it over into what's called a *1031 Exchange,* into another property, and defer the taxes from that point forward on the property. As long as you're buying real estate, you're able to continue with the tax benefits and defer your gains all the way through. Cash flow is a powerful advantage of real estate if you understand how to do it.

Appreciation

The next advantage is appreciation. I like to say the first reason you should buy real estate is for cash flow. However, the biggest money is made in appreciation because you are controlling such a large asset with a little bit of your own money. In the illustrations we have been using, we are putting a 10% down payment on a $100,000 property. Let me give you an example of the power of appreciation.

Let's say you start investing in real estate and every year for 10 years you purchase one property. In year one, you've acquired this $100,000 property. The appreciation on this property at just 5% would be $5,000 at the end of the year. If we had a loan, the 30-year loan we talked about at 8% interest, the equity buy-down (the principal you would have paid down) would have been about $800. Your total equity at the end of year one would be the $5,000 in appreciation plus the equity buy-down of $800. You would now have a total increase in your property of $5,800.

Let's say we jump to year three in this example. Now, you have three properties at $300,000. Your appreciation at the end of that year on those three properties would be $31,000, approximately. Your equity buy-down on those three properties would be around $5,200. Your total increase for the year would be $36,000. So, you can see how it begins to escalate as you begin to increase the amount of properties you own.

Then, we can move all the way out to year seven. If you've bought a property every year, you've got $700,000 in property value. Your appreciation on those properties is $155,000. Your equity buy-down has increased to $27,600 because it keeps increasing every year from the other properties. Now you have an equity of $182,000. Then, in year 10 you've acquired 10 properties. You now have $1,000,000 in properties. Your appreciation has built up because you have 10 properties that have been appreciating over these last 10 years. Now, you're at $320,800 just with 5% appreciation a year. Your equity buy-down has increased all the way up to about $60,000, so you're at about $380,000 just by buying one property a year.

You can see how fast your equity position in property can increase with appreciation and equity buy-down. At the end of 10 years, just with these conservative numbers, you're at $380,000 of increased value.

But let's say that you become a little more aggressive. You decide that you are going to buy three properties a year. Instead of buying one $100,000 property, you are going to purchase three $100,000 properties. You appreciate at 5% a year on that investment, and your equity buy-down is to be determined on a 30-year mortgage at 8% interest.

If you bought three houses at $100,000 each that were worth $300,000, you would have $15,000 in appreciation that year. You would have an equity buy-down of around $2,500, which means you would have around $17,500 in total equity at the end of the first year. That doesn't sound like a lot, but that's just on the appreciation and equity buy-down.

If you carry that principle all the way out to five years and you've bought those three properties every year, you will get all the way up to about $1,000,000. At the end of five years, you will get to $1,500,000. Your appreciation would be $240,000, and your equity buy-down would be about $42,000. You would end up with about $282,000 just at the end of that year accumulated. You carry that all the way out to year 10, and you would then have $3,000,000 worth of property. Your appreciation would be $960,000, and your equity buy-down would be $178,000. That would total $1,100,000. Just through appreciation and equity buy-down, you would become a millionaire.

I am inserting the appreciation chart here once again so you can visualize a little easier.

Year	Property Value	Appreciation	Equity Buy Down	Total Equity
1	$100,000	$5,000	$800	$5,800
3	$300,000	$31,100	$5,200	$36,000
5	$500,000	$80,300	$13,900	$94,200
7	$700,000	$155,000	$27,600	$182,600
10	$1,100,000	$320,800	$59,400	$379,400

Year	Property Value	Appreciation	Equity Buy Down	Total Equity
1	$300,000	$15,000	$2,400	$17,400
3	$600,000	$93,300	$15,600	$108,900
5	$1,500,000	$240,900	$41,700	$282,600
7	$2,100,000	$465,000	$82,800	$547,800
10	$3,000,000	$960,000	$178,200	$1,138,200

Tax Benefits

The next reason that I really like real estate is because of the tax benefits. As I mentioned, whenever you are figuring your returns on real estate, you must include the tax benefits. A lot of people fail to do this.

I had people recently tell me they paid $120,000 in taxes in the first quarter alone. They prepaid on their taxes. I thought about the real estate we could have bought with that, and how we could have sheltered those taxes.

One of the tax benefits you get is depreciation. You get to deduct approximately 1/27th of the value of the property, not counting the land. The loss of depreciation goes directly against any kind of profit or gains that you had on the property. You're able to also deduct the interest that you're paying on the home loan. In the next few paragraphs, I will explain a particular designation you can get to save you tens of thousands of dollars on your taxes, Or, if you are a Donald Trump, it can save you tens of millions of dollars on your taxes.

It is a tax designation for real estate investors that will classify you as a full-time **real estate professional.** Beginner real estate investors should work toward this designation. Basically, it says that if you spend 750 hours a year on your real estate investments and you own your real estate business, then you can receive the full benefit of your tax exemptions. Currently, the IRS will limit your deductions to $25,000 annually if you do not have this designation. If you make $100,000 or more, it will disappear at $150,000.

In other words, if you have $150,000 of taxable income, you will not receive deductions unless you receive this designation.

As you begin to build your real estate business, keep this in mind. If you combine "buying and holding" with "buying and flipping" or "wholesaling," then this designation will become easier to get. I have a student who purchased a six-unit building and because he was always looking for bargain deals and did not have the cash to buy the properties, he would raise cash by wholesaling to other investors. His wholesaling business grew, and in his first year of investing, he received the real estate professional designation on his taxes.

Also, there is what's called a *1031 Exchange.* You are able to pay no capital gains on properties when you sell them by putting them into a 1031 Exchange. This is called *rolling over your gains into another like-kind property,* and no taxes have to be paid. The federal government capital gains rate is 15%. In the state that I live in, the state capital gains rate is 5%. If I sell a property after a year and I make a capital gain, let's say of $100,000, I would owe $20,000 on an investment property.

However, your primary residence can be even better for your taxes. If you make a capital gains profit of up to $500,000 on your own house, there are no taxes since it is your primary residence.

To reclassify a property as your primary residence, you have to live in it for at least two out of the last five years. You actually can take a $500,000 capital gains exemption on two different properties. So, you can make $1,000,000 from two houses if each is considered your primary residence in two of the last five years.

You get a capital gains exemption for investors, the 1031 Exchange, and then you get the resident exemption on capital gains for your primary residence.

Control

Another advantage of owning real estate is control. When we buy stock, we have no control. In real estate, you can purchase below market value for instant equity if you know what you're doing. I have done this more times than I can count. In fact, I do not purchase a property unless I'm moving in with instant equity.

I have a contract on an investment property right now that I bought for $340,000. The identical property next to it sold for $430,000.

This property was in the same condition. It needed no rehab, no work, no anything. A lot of times, the situation of the seller is what determines whether or not I can buy below market value. A couple of years ago, I bought a similar property for around 27% less than the original purchase price. It was in a luxury area, and I sold that property a year later for a tremendous profit. You can purchase below market value for instant equity for control.

You can also create value through rehab. I can change the way the property looks by fixing it up, adding shutters, painting it, adding carpet, and so much more. There are many things I can do to create value. If you buy below market value and then you create value, you can sell or rent for way more than what you invested in the property. For example, if you bought a property at 20% below market, created value that adds another 20%, that adds up to 40% in added value for more control.

Insurance

Another thing I like about real estate is that it can be insured. It can be insured against losses or litigation. We'll go over legal matters and how to set up what we call a *limited liability company (LLC) tree* to protect yourself later. You can insure your property against natural disasters and many other forms of damage, which means your investment is pretty secure.

Creative Financing

Another reason I like real estate is that you have the opportunity to use other people's money. The first way to do this is to bring in a partner who will put all the money into the deal. He or she will provide the down payment, costs for rehab or whatever is needed, and then you both split the profits. Think about that. You won't be using your money or your credit. Instead, you're using an investor, and you've formed a simple partnership to be able to purchase the property.

There are other ways to use people's money too. You can take advantage of a lease option in which you lease a property from a person who is trying to sell it. You and that person agree on the lease payment, and then you tie an option with that lease so once you get control of the property you can start fixing it up. You can then lease option it to another person, or in some cases, lease option and then flip it to another investor. There are a lot of ways to do it, but the point is you're not using any of your own money or your own credit if you know how to lease option creatively.

You can also do a wholesale flip. This is when you find properties, and instead of having any kind of transaction with a title company, you can just flip it over to another investor and get a finder's fee.

There is power in what you're able to accomplish in real estate.

CHAPTER 4

HOW TO IDENTIFY THE BEST MARKETS TO BUY

I want to start off by qualifying this statement: A market does not have to meet these criteria for you to find a good property, but it will weigh the odds heavily in your favor.

Property Prices

The first way we can identify a good market is when property prices are not more than two to three times the median income. For an example, let's consider Colorado Springs, Colorado. In 2009, the median income there was $52,000. Property prices, according to this rule of thumb, should be no more than three times the median income, which would be $156,000. Next, we would research the median property price, which for this example was $183,000. The median property price is more than three times the median income, which means that if we're not careful, we can get into an overheated market in Colorado Springs.

To provide another example, let's look at Portsmouth, Virginia. The median income was $48,000, and the median property price was $129,000. Then, $48,000 times three would be $144,000. Based on this criterion, Portsmouth, Virginia, would be a good place to potentially look at purchasing property because the median income is greater than the median price. That means the median house is going to catch up to the median income at some point.

You can still make money buying properties and renting them in a market that is four to five times higher if you know what you're doing. If the income is high, then rents will also be high. For example, you could own multiple houses in Salt Lake City but not live in Salt Lake City. The price of those houses, therefore, would not be based on your income. They would be in the sense that you would be borrowing money from the banks and buying houses in Salt Lake City, but the source of money that is buying those houses would not be coming from earnings in that area.

Rent

The next way to identify a good market is to research how strong the rents are in the area and what drives them. The monthly rents must be no less than 1-1.5% of the purchase price. So, for a $100,000 house, the least amount you want to get for rent is $1,000.

You want to go as high up in property value as you can go in the current market. I would rather buy a higher-end property if I can afford it and get a 1% gross return than I would a lower-end property and get a 1.5% return, all things being equal.

Here's an additional observation. As I am writing, interest rates are at such historical lows that a $100,000 property that rents for $800 per month (.08 per month) could work because you are paying less in interest. That means more money goes into your pocket. In fact, the 1.0 -1.5% rule was really created as a guideline when interest rates were around 7% to 8%. Higher-priced properties, where at least a 20% down payment is used and financed at current low rates will have good positive return most of the time.

Housing Supply

The next way to identify a balanced market is by housing supply. A good market should have about six months' worth, where supply means the number of houses listed. This means it's got the right number of buyers and sellers in the market.

In order to calculate supply, take the number of houses currently for sale and divide by the number of houses that sold last month. The result is the number of months it would take to sell the inventory of houses currently for sale. Three months of inventory is a hot market (seller's market). Six months of inventory is a balanced market (equal for buyers and sellers). Nine months of inventory means the market is soft (buyer's market). I like to buy when the trend is moving from a soft market to a balanced market.

Job Growth

The fourth indicator of a good market is that job growth is taking place. You don't want a boom or bust cycle like in the oil industry. You want to find consistent job growth happening. That means the real estate market will have value and, in an ideal world, that property taxes are low.

For example, Texas has no state income tax, but their property taxes are atrocious. So, when I'm buying in Pittsburgh, Texas, I have to stay closer to 1.5% on any property including higher up the scale because the property taxes will hammer me.

Formulas in Overheated Markets

After making some good money a while ago, I moved to The Woodlands, Texas, and bought a few Great Clips hair salons. I didn't manage them; I just wanted to invest some money.

I already had a home down in that area, so my wife didn't want to buy another one. I told her to find an apartment she liked for us to rent. She looked at a two-bedroom apartment right in the heart of The Woodlands, but they wanted $2,200 a month for it. I thought they had lost their minds, so I told my wife to find a townhouse.

She found a couple of brownstones she liked, so I called the guy renting out the brownstone and told him I was interested in renting. I offered to pay a year's worth of rent upfront and asked for the best price he could give me. He said the best he could do was $4,200 a month. I asked if rent was really that high in this area, and he confirmed it.

I called up a realtor friend of mine and asked how much I would have to pay for a nice place, and he said $5,000-$6,000 a month. I went to look at a property, and it was $7,500 a month to rent. So I began to run the numbers in my head. For single-family, high-end properties, people were getting 1-1.2% in rent. That was a lot of money.

I realized I was sitting on a gold mine. I felt like a blind hog finding an acorn. My wife didn't want me to buy a house, but I teach this stuff all the time. It was too good of an opportunity, so I paid cash for a house 30 days later. It was an incredibly nice place, and when I sold it, I made a killing.

My wife didn't want to live in Houston, so I sold the hair franchises and got my money back. She wanted to sell our other properties, but I told her we should see what we could get for rent. I listed our properties for rent, and a realtor called me to say he had a cash offer. In fact, a man wanted to pay all his rent upfront for one year.

I was putting a ton of money in my pocket every month with no expense. It was a lot of money. I made sure to get 1-1.5% back in rent and at least $300/month in positive cash flow.

There are good markets anywhere you go. At the writing of this book, the market in Denver, Colorado, is hot. Supply is low, prices are high, and the job market is expanding. However, you can find pockets of cooler markets around Colorado.

I remember one woman came to my real estate workshop one year and told me that she appreciated my teaching, but she was sure she couldn't find any houses that matched the formulas I taught her. I told her to talk to a realtor. A few months later, she contacted my office and told me that to her own surprise she had found houses that aligned with the formula. You may be skeptical, and that's okay. But let me encourage you to finish reading this book and then see what you can find!

CHAPTER 5

KEYS TO FINDING BARGAIN PROPERTIES

The most important thing you need to understand is how to find properties that already have value when you acquire them. In order for you to understand how to find bargain properties, I'm going to outline some key tips and strategies.

Key 1: Know What You Want

First, you must establish clearly what you desire to accomplish. This allows you to know what properties to say no to. There will be plenty of properties that are good investments, but they may not necessarily be good for you. That's why it's important that you clearly establish what you want to achieve.

I remember looking at several haircutting franchises a couple of years ago, and I began to run the numbers on them. I found out that I could buy a certain brand that allowed absentee management. At the time, however, I was aggressively involved in real estate investing. When I began to examine the returns, I saw that the returns were much better for me in the real estate arena where I already had the team and the systems in place. I purchased several of the franchises to experiment but learned that my return on cash was much better in real estate.

People have different objectives for what they want to achieve. Some people want to get out of debt, others need money for their children's education, others want to retire in comfort. Let me give you advice that will help you when it comes to investing. A great goal that will clearly establish what you want is simply this: Replace your current income.

What is it you have to do through investing to replace your current income? That's what we are referring to when we talk about reaching financial independence through passive income. We spelled it out in the first two chapters of the book. It is owning assets that pay you income every month. Even though buying and selling real estate is a good strategy for producing more immediate income, we really want to focus on buying and holding for rental income that replaces your current job income.

When you start understanding that as your goal, it begins to clarify what you're looking for. Again, number one on the list is to establish clearly what you desire to accomplish.

Key 2: Play the Numbers Game

When considering what properties to purchase, it's important that you physically go look at them. This helps you to learn to evaluate properties and determine what kind of repairs they will need. Once you have learned firsthand, then you can begin to rely on real estate agents to look at them for you. With the ability to FaceTime, agents can give you a live tour with their phone. This allows you to see many properties without having to go yourself. You can have an agent pre-screen them based on the formula that you give them. When you find one that matches what you are looking for, you still have to crunch the numbers for yourself. Finding bargain properties is a time investment to evaluate based on the property's condition and what kind rental income it will produce.

Some people say you have to look at 100 properties to purchase one good one. I can tell you what my experience has been in real-life real estate investing. Once I give a real estate agent the formula I'm adhering to, they show me properties that align with it. The formula is this: the purchase investment needs to be no more than 80% of the *as-repaired* value of the property. (In today's low interest environment, you can pay up to 90% or more of as-repaired value and still have cash flow). I also would want a $300 a month spread (positive cash flow) after principal, interest, taxes, and insurance.

Let me say this just as a quick note: don't become emotionally attached to properties. If the numbers don't work, they don't work. Don't try to make them work. Just move on and start looking at another property. There will always be other properties.

You can put a system on the ground with a real estate agent that will allow you to leverage your time, so you don't have to spend as much time looking. Let the agent pre-screen the properties for you, so you only look at the best deals.

Key 3: Focus on Residential Properties

The next step is to focus on residential properties, primarily single-family ones. The advantage is that they can be bought with a regular purchase, non-commercial mortgage. This gives you the greatest advantage.

Here's why. First of all, it's a lower cost to enter. Typically, when you're looking at single-family homes, the price you can actually purchase the property for is less than a small apartment building. Obviously, with a small apartment building you get more units, but single-family homes are great for learning real estate investing because the entry costs are lower, and the management is easier. There is less money down, and it's easier to purchase a $100,000 house than a $500,000 apartment building. If you want to scale up later, you can bring in partners. Also, single-family houses don't have to be sold to other investors. People are looking for a place to live so someone may purchase your single-family investment property as their primary home. Most of the time, people purchasing a property for their primary home are willing to pay more than other investors. Small apartment buildings are purchased only by other investors.

Key 4: Look for Distressed Properties

Distressed means the physical condition of the property. This is important because you want to buy properties for less than you know the real value would be. You will know the real value of the property is more than the price because of the location of the property, the size of the property, or "fixing it up" to increase the value.

It is best to purchase a property that needs only cosmetic improvement. To be able to determine if a property is a good deal, it's important that you have some idea about how to inspect a property. In order to do this, you need to find a quality professional inspector and get a written report. I can't tell you how many times that has kept me out of serious trouble. I have tried to bypass that. I have tried to use less expensive inspectors. In some cases, I've tried to just use the contractor who's going to do the repairs as the inspector, which is a tremendous mistake. You want that third-party opinion so it is unbiased. Then, get a second opinion with your contractor.

Key 5: Determining Value

There are a couple ways to determine the value of a property. The first one is looking for what similar properties in an area have sold for. Keep in mind, you're looking for actual sales prices, not just the list prices.

Another way to determine value is to look at replacement costs. In other words, what would it cost to rebuild the house that you're looking at? Are you getting it at a good price within that range?

The last one is simply income. What kind of income will the house produce for you? When you're looking at the income of a house, you're always looking for positive cash flow. That's what helps you evaluate. You want to look for a 1.5% monthly return on each property. For example, if the total cost of the house is $100,000, you want a 1.5% monthly return. So, you're looking to get $1,500 per month in rent out of that property.

You might have to end up keeping a property and holding it for longer than you thought, so you want to make sure you can actually get rents that will put money in your pocket.

Key 6: Look at the Seller

In my opinion, I think this is the key to finding good bargains in real estate. Some people say it's location, location, location. There is no doubt that location is critical when talking about value. However, you make money in real estate when you buy, not when you sell. The seller is the number-one key to a property being a good deal.

Usually, you'll know if the situation of a seller is distressed by the listing price of the property. For example, if I'm looking at properties in a certain neighborhood that are all listed at $100,000, and I come across one property listed for $75,000, my antennas go up.

Is it too small? Is it the condition of the property? In some cases, it's a combination of both—the property is a little run-down and the seller is very motivated.

Sometimes, the property owners are out-of-town owners who don't want to hassle with the house. They may have received the property through an inheritance. Divorce is another good example of someone being motivated and willing to sell the house at a discount. You don't want to take advantage of people, but sometimes couples are trying to settle the situation they're in. They need to be able to get rid of the house, so you're helping them by doing that. Sometimes, you just have owners who are tired of a property and want out, so there is a higher degree of motivation to unload the property. One of my favorites is an estate sale where relatives of a deceased person are selling a property. Many times they don't want to spend a lot of time on trying to sell a house so they respond with low price to the first strong buyer who comes along.

Key 7: Foreclosures

There is a lot spoken and written about foreclosures, but I want to try to help you understand foreclosures better. A foreclosure is when the person who has borrowed money for the property has not paid their loan payment in a timely manner. The lender will send out a letter telling the borrower the foreclosure process will begin if the borrower does not respond and catch it up. If the borrower doesn't catch up, then the property goes back to the lender who must offer it at a public auction.

I don't like public actions for foreclosures simply because many times the bank is there bidding against you to drive the price up. Typically, they also don't give you enough time to really examine the property and make a good decision. I like to buy foreclosures after they have become what's called *real estate owned (REO)* by that particular lender.

You miss some deals in doing it this way, but you usually have more room to negotiate on a particular property because the lenders are not in the business of owning real estate. They're in the business of loaning money.

Foreclosures are a good way to buy properties at discounts because lenders want to unload the properties themselves. I believe the best way to buy a foreclosure is once the lender—whether it's a government agency or private bank—has actually taken the property back. That's what you want to see because you can negotiate better at that point. With this approach on foreclosures, you don't have to take a "foreclosure seminar." You just wait for properties to come up that meet your formulas for buying, and if the property happens to be a foreclosure, then that's great.

Key 8: Identifying Your Formula

When I'm looking for a bargain property, the first thing I consider is the price. I want a total investment of no more than 80% of as-repaired value. That includes my acquisition cost, my purchase price, my repair costs, my carrying costs, and possibly my selling cost if I have to pay a real estate commission. I still want to be no more than 80% of real value. That protects me and the property.

Let me give you a good nugget here: the tax assessment is sometimes a good purchase point. A property will be assessed for about 20% less than it's really worth. One of the guidelines I use to determine whether a property is a good deal is whether or not I can purchase the property around the tax assessment.

You also want to compare the property you're looking at to similar properties. If I'm looking in the neighborhood of $100,000 houses generally selling for $100,000, I want to buy something at that $75,000-$80,000 mark.

Then, look at the rents. The gross monthly rent returns should be 1.5% on the total investment of the property. A property that sells for $50,000 should return $750 a month in gross rents. A property that is worth $100,000 should be $1,500 in gross rent. That's 1.5%. You can get by with 1%, but the margins are a lot tighter there. So you have to be a lot more careful. The positive cash flow should be $300 per month. That's after principal, interest, taxes, insurance, and management fee. The least you should ever go down to is about $150. If you want to manage the property yourself, then that's ok on your first several properties. But you shouldn't spend all your time on managing if you are still building your portfolio. You should spend your time finding new properties.

The principal and interest amount is based on a 30-year loan at the current interest rate. When you factor that in, then you add taxes, insurance, and possibly a management fee. A management fee is usually somewhere between 7-10%. Understanding the basic rental numbers of a property helps you determine the value and identify bargain properties. Look at the price, rent, and the neighborhood.

Most of the time, best cash flow comes from low-to-moderate income neighborhoods. There are a few rare exceptions to this. But for the most part, if you're looking for cash flow in property—and frankly, appreciation will be a little slower—the low-to-moderate income neighborhoods are the best. There is a low entry point as far as costs, and you would be simply amazed sometimes at how high rents can be in these neighborhoods. Sometimes the rents are close to the same amount as a three-bedroom house in a nicer neighborhood.

I'll give you an example. I bought a house. I paid $32,000 for a single family three-bedroom 1.5 bath brick attached townhome on the East Coast. My total cost for that property was less than $40,000. I rented that property for $800 per month. My positive cash flow was $515 a month. I had no repairs or vacancies for several years, so I earned good rental from that property.

Some people want to stay away from low-income neighborhoods. I'm not suggesting that you purchase a property at any level in crime-ridden neighborhoods. What I am suggesting is you look at some of the fringes of those low-to-moderate income neighborhoods and focus there. You have to have a good management system in place in order to make money, but it's key that you have and maintain strong cash flow spreads.

Let's talk about the next one—value. You want to be 70-80% into a property, if possible. In other words, you want to buy a property at 20-30% less than what the total value is. I see people in Colorado buying properties for 105% of what it's worth. The truth is, you get burned doing that over and over and over again. If you can't buy a property for less than it is worth, then you're probably trying to buy in the wrong market.

Key 9: Real Estate Agents

I would like to close this chapter by focusing on the importance of using real estate agents. There are all kinds of ways to find bargain properties, but in my opinion, the best way is to use real estate agents who are investors themselves. Put more time into finding a real estate agent that understands investing because of his ownership of investment properties. I always tell agents that we can buy as many properties as they can find that fits the formula. You may not be able to do that just yet, but keep striving for it. I made several good agents the top agents of the year in their particular areas because of the amount of properties we purchased.

As I stated, one of the keys to finding good real estate agents is to ask them if they own investment properties themselves and for how long. You cannot waste your time with a retail agent.

Secondly, ask them if they work with any rehab contractors. They probably have good connections with contractors who will work for good prices and do quality work.

Then, ask the prospective real estate agent if they or another agent they know personally manages a property. That's a key because management can be the Achilles' heel in building wealth in real estate. You've got to have good management.

Number four, when you meet with the agent, explain your formula and ask the agent to bring you only properties that meet it. That's huge! Make the agent sit down with a piece of paper and figure it out. Remember, you make money in real estate when you buy, not when you sell.

Avoid inexperienced agents who have what I call *commission breath.* In other words, all they're looking for is a quick sale; they're not really looking for a long-term relationship with an investor. Also, avoid retail agents. These are people who know how to do retail deals pretty well, but they are lost doing investor deals. You want somebody who will understand an investor's needs.

Spend more time looking for an investor agent than you do for properties. If you find an agent who has access to the MLS and you give him or her your formula, you can leverage your time, your eyes, and your ears exponentially. Find someone you trust who knows the formula and then you'll know that when they bring you properties that meet the formula, you will want to buy them.

Let them use their resources to do the work for you. In fact, here is one of the major keys of this entire program: Learn to spend time getting a team on the ground and understand the importance of having an investor agent.

I hear people teaching in tougher markets that you have to sometimes look for seller ads in newspapers for "Sale by Owner" signs. Of course, I like working the Department of Housing and Urban Development (HUD) foreclosures and going personally to REO departments, printing business cards that say "I buy real estate!" But here's the truth of the matter, if you will use an agent to screen properties for you, your time can be leveraged so much.

You can look at 100 properties in the time somebody else is looking at two, So, again, I encourage you to spend your time looking for a good real estate agent.

CHAPTER 6

14 MISTAKES INVESTORS MAKE

Any time we begin any endeavor, especially a business endeavor, we're going to make mistakes. The key is to learn from mistakes so they become a process of noble failure. In other words, we must *fail forward*. This means after learning from our mistakes, we move ahead smarter and stronger in our businesses and our lives. We use these mistakes as springboards to advance us, so we can develop passive income through owning real estate.

Mistake 1: Waiting to Get in the Game

The first mistake I see new investors make in real estate investing is to start later rather than sooner. The sooner you get started, the greater your knowledge base becomes.

I heard a man say years ago, that most people live and die in a non-growth environment. How true. They never put themselves in a place where they have to stretch, and they never "get in the game." The sooner you get in the game of real estate investing, the more it will help you in different areas of your life. Obviously, you will learn how to make money instead of just earn money. Therefore, even if you lose everything, you still know how to make it back.

If you start sooner rather than later, you are able to increase your wealth even more because you will gain more assets and get the benefit of income as well as the growth and the appreciation of those assets. The rule of 72 states is that at 20% interest, your money would double every five years. The idea is that the longer you can hold the assets, the more increase you have in your net worth as well as your ability to have a greater income stream.

So, waiting or starting later really is a mistake. You need to get in the game and learn how to play it. Some people have "analysis paralysis," and they never move forward. They never pull the trigger, so to speak. Getting in the game helps you know how to hold the ball and throw the ball. Bottom line, you learn how to make money.

I do want to add an important thought here. Even though earlier is definitely better, it's never too late to start investing. If you're nearing retirement or just looking to get out of your day job, there's no time like the present. The sooner you can start, the better off you are!

Mistake 2: Lack of Focus

The second mistake new investors make is not focusing their energy on what will make them money. What I mean by that is when you look at properties, it's absolutely imperative that you review the deals. In other words, if you have an agent bring you pre-screened deals, you should look at properties and deals every week. Every single week you should be looking at new deals to determine if the numbers are there.

Focus your attention on crunching the numbers. When you're considering different properties, evaluate them based on the questions I have posed in this book. *Am I getting in this property for no more than a total of 80% of its real value? Does it offer cash flow? Is there $300 positive cash flow per month on a single-family home?*

When you can answer yes to the above questions, then spend your time actually writing contracts. Focus your energy on what will make money and write contracts where you know you will make money. Remember, you make money when you buy, not when you sell. The more contracts you write based on the model we have prescribed, the more likely one will be accepted.

Mistake 3: Not Maintaining a Cash Reserve

Real estate is a very cash-intensive business, and it's easy to run out of cash. When you put money down on a property, that money is tied up in that property until you refinance it or sell it. In addition, money for repairs also can be invested depending on how you structure the loans (which we'll look at a little later).

It's not just a matter of having negative cash flow on properties, but even with positive cash flow you still must manage your cash reserves.

New investors use all their reserves and make down payments and repairs. That's why I encourage you to work with a real estate agent who knows what investors need. A helpful agent who knows your cash situation can be a reliable sounding board to bounce off ideas.

Here are my best tips for never running out of liquid cash. First, keep some uncommitted cash. Secondly, maintain an untouchable account. Lock it up somewhere. Whenever you're doing loans for refinances, to be able to pull money out of your other properties, the lender requires at least six months cash of reserves for the loan payment on that particular property. You want to maintain some untouchable money, and not run out of cash. Make sure your rental income from your properties is still flowing. If you run out of cash, then you stop the whole train because you can't get approved for refinancing.

Along with keeping untouchable amounts of cash, check your credit score every month or so. There are three credit bureaus, so you have three credit scores. Most lenders go with your "middle score" but continually monitor and manage your score.

Keep a pulse on your properties, and watch as they go up in value so that you can refinance before you need it. In other words, do not let yourself get backed into a corner where you run out of cash. You may have to pull money out of a property and put it in your untouchable account so you can keep investing.

Managing your actual cash and your reserve cash and overseeing your cash flow and credit is a constant requirement for the active investor. These things need to be properly managed all the time, so you maintain cash coming into your real estate business.

Mistake 4: Flying Solo

The next mistake I see from new investors is overlooking having a good team and systems on the ground. This is one of the greatest challenges especially when you're buying real estate outside of where you live, but it's also just as true when you buy it in the immediate area of your own home.

The first team member you must have is a real estate agent. Find a real estate agent who does not have "commission breath" and is not just a retail agent but one who understands investors.

The second team member you need is a solid, dependable, and economical contractor for your rehabs and repairs. You probably need more than one, and they have to be fast and available in order for you to make money.

The third team member you need is a property manager to buy and hold property. I'm a huge advocate of working with property managers as opposed to managing property yourself. A major reason is if you manage the property, you will end up sacrificing a lot of time you could spend actually finding deals. Let me add a caveat here: If you're a first-time investor, it's important for you to learn to manage the first few properties yourself, and then look for a property manager.

The fourth team member you need is a good mortgage broker who understands investor loans, just like your real estate agent. The way most "broker shops" work is that they broker the loans to lenders. Many of them end up only working with only three to four different lenders. If the broker is not out shopping the products, it can become very limited. They will tell you, "I can only do four properties for you," or "I can only do 10," or whatever their number is. The primary reason they are limited is because of the quasi-government lending institutions like Freddie Mac or Fannie Mae that allow mortgage brokers to only make a certain number of investor loans. However, there are other large mortgage bond programs that will allow more loans than Freddie or Fannie. The mortgage brokers sometimes are telling more about themselves than they are about you, specifically in your financial condition. They just don't have access to other products. So, you need to find a mortgage broker who is knowledgeable and experienced when working with investors and understands how to find particular loans.

The fifth team member you need is a banker. I'm big on having a banker especially if I want to move quickly on deals. For example, if I want to flip a property, I typically will not use an actual mortgage product. I will use a local bank, typically a community bank, and have them loan me money. We will then work out the parameters with them on the loan-to-value on the property. That loan-to-value is the size of the loan to the appraised value of the property. The local banks are typically much more flexible than any of the mortgage products, especially if you're going to buy property and flip it.

That loan is usually good for six months to three years depending on the bank. You can obviously renew them, but I typically refinance with a mortgage broker, take the money I put in that project out, and then move onto another one. I have several banks set up so I can have several projects going on at the same time.

The sixth team member you must have is a good insurance agent who understands investor properties and how the property needs to be covered. For example, in all areas where I had properties, I used an umbrella-type of liability policy, hazard insurance and, in some cases, flood insurance on each one of the houses. I try to stay out of the flood areas, but I do have a property or two that needed flood insurance. You need an insurance agent who understands the insurance products just like you need a mortgage broker who understands the mortgage products.

The seventh team member you need is an accountant. I just can't say this enough. Accounting is huge in order to understand how to account for your expenses. An example would be spending money on a roof. Is it a repair or is it a capital expenditure? That definitely affects you because if it's a capital expenditure, it changes the cost basis on your property. It allows you to have more depreciation as you move forward.

The eighth team member you need is an attorney, and this will be one of the most significant members of your team. One of the things that we use in our real estate holdings is what's called an *LLC tree*. We use an LLC tree around each property, a single-member LLC. Then my wife and I have a dual member LLC that we both equally own, and all the single member LLCs flow into that. We also have a trust that's above that owned by that master dual member LLC. (We'll talk more about LLCs in Chapter 11: "Legal Matters in Real Estate.")

This protects you and your holdings. If you were to get sued on a particular property, the only thing at risk would be the property that is in that LLC. Usually, it's not at risk because you have insurance as your first barrier, so you're well protected most of the time. Having an attorney as a part of your team is absolutely critical.

I want to really encourage you to get these team members: real estate agent, contractors, mortgage broker, property manager, banker, insurance agent, accountant, and attorney.

Mistake 5: Not Consulting a Professional

The next mistake I see newcomers make is not obtaining professional opinions on everything, especially on property values. Appraisers often tell me the value of a property, but if I disagree with the appraiser, I will order a second appraisal just to make sure. The three most important words in business are verify, verify, verify.

I had a property where the roof estimates ranged from $7,500 to $20,000. I asked for detailed printed estimates, and I found out the lowest bid guy was right on the money. Then, I reviewed the specifics of what kind of materials they were putting on and what process they were using to install them. I checked that against the next guy up on the roofing bid and the next guy. Verifying the information lets me know that I'm actually getting what I'm paying for. When you receive information, make sure that you verify and get everything you can in writing. If it's not in writing, it doesn't count.

Mistake 6: Bypassing Low-to-Moderate Neighborhoods

The next mistake is bypassing the low-to-moderate income neighborhoods. This is where your best cash flow spread is. Typically, management is more intensive, but the cash flows are so much better in these kinds of neighborhoods.

Appreciation is good, relatively speaking. If you buy houses right, your rents typically are going to be good as well. If the houses are in pretty decent shape and you have decent tenants, they are easily flipped to other investors.

Mistake 7: Single-Source Financing

The next mistake is failing to establish multiple sources of financing. As I mentioned before, you need to have more than one broker. The reason is that mortgage brokers typically work with different lenders, usually only with three to four. Mortgage brokers get paid better by the lenders that they do the most volume with. What's called a *yield spread* becomes better the more business they do with a particular lender. This could affect you negatively because they're not out shopping for other products for you to get you the best deal.

I also like to have at least two bankers per each area where I am buying real estate, so I have different resources. This way, you will not run out of places to find money. We call it *real estate,* but really, it's *finance estate* because if you can't get the properties financed, it's impossible to do real estate deals.

One of the biggest mistakes is failing to establish multiple sources of financing. Again, I want to stress knowing your credit score before every deal. You have to know where you are. Sometimes you don't even know certain things are on your report that may have affected it.

An example would be if you refinanced a few properties at a time. When those refinances all hit your credit, they will knock down your score. Perhaps the most important advice I could give you is to never be 30 days late on paying your bills.

Mistake 8: Cutting Down the Tree

The pecan orchard story that I shared with you in the introduction is really applicable here. If you were to cut down your trees for firewood, you would have no more pecans. This is the difference between vegetables and fruit. Many vegetables have to be killed to actually eat them. Think of broccoli or cabbage. Whereas fruit trees never have to be killed in order to eat the fruit. They just keep producing fruit year after year. This is what happens when you sell a property. You are able to "eat" the cash flow now, but for the future, there is no more cash flow because you don't own it anymore. By selling you can end up killing the goose that lays the golden eggs.

We also discussed earlier the subject of appreciation—that you receive the appreciation on the entire value of the property, not just what you invested. For example, if you put $10,000 in a $100,000 house, the appreciation you receive is on the entire $100,000, not just on the $10,000 you put in. What's powerful is if you refinance to get back the $10,000 down payment, you are able to put the $10,000 directly in your pocket. Now, you have no money in that property, so the return on your investment is basically infinite because you never put anything in it to start with, so to speak. You received your money back out. The longer you hold the asset, the more you're going to earn.

Remember this: a house will double in value approximately every 12 years. If you have a $100,000 house, you hold it for 12 years and your tenants are paying the mortgage and the cost of the house, you just made $100,000 in 12 years. When you begin to add that up with the tax benefits and the positive cash flow, the return becomes fairly substantial. The people who have become the wealthiest in real estate are people who have held properties.

In other words, they didn't cut down their fruit trees for firewood, but they continued to harvest the fruit year after year. They are taking the cash flow and allowing the appreciation to build wealth long term.

Mistake 9: Getting Emotionally Attached

One of the greatest mistakes that newcomers make is overpaying for properties. Several years ago, I made a deal on a luxury condo in a ski area where I paid the lowest price per square foot that had ever been paid for a two-bedroom condo.

When I first started making the offer, I had people telling me it couldn't be done, but we stuck with our guns and made a historical buy. Again, remember: you make money when you buy, not when you sell. Do not become emotionally tied to a property. Instead, look at the numbers!

You can also become emotionally tied to a property and over-rehab it. You have to make sure you can get money from the added value that you're putting in, and it has to at least cover those costs. An example would be putting granite countertops in a kitchen where the neighborhood itself does not typically have granite countertops. Today, granite countertops are becoming commonplace, however, you still don't want to spend money on over-rehabbing a property because it makes you feel better.

Remember, if it's an investment property, you're not the one who will be living there, your tenant is. You need a nice, clean, neat property for your tenants, but don't overpay for it.

Stick with your formulas, and if what you're looking at does not fit the formula, then do not purchase it. Be willing to walk away from any deal—that's the greatest negotiating position you have! Never get yourself emotionally tied to a property where you're unable to walk away. Let the numbers tell you the story, not the color of the paint or how the plants smell. Make sure you're look-ing at the numbers, and that will keep you in the driver's seat during negotiations.

Mistake 10: Not Enough Cash Flow

Then the next mistake is not creating enough cash flow from your rentals. When you are buying and holding property, the tar-get formula is $300 positive cash flow per month after principal, interest, taxes, insurance, and management.

If you're not creating enough cash flow from your rentals, nega-tive cash flow is possible because you will have some repairs. Your goal on repairs is not to have more than 5% of the gross monthly rent go out to repairs. Your goal is also not to have more than 5% vacancy. If you add those two 5% up, that's 10% of your gross rent. That's a small margin, but it is possible to achieve and even exceed if the property is competently and resourcefully managed.

I encourage you to establish a repair sheet cost ahead of time. When the tenant moves into the property, take this repair sheet with the costs written on it. Put all of the repairs down, go through the property when a tenant moves in, and establish that every-thing has been repaired. You are covered, and the tenant knows ahead of time what the repair would cost if damage happens, and then that tenant is responsible for those repairs.

If something goes wrong, you have to fix it. However, if you have a repair sheet with all repair costs outlined when their rent comes due the next month, they'll know how much extra they would be charged. If a tenant's rent is $850 a month and they had a stopped-up toilet, they now owe $925 for this coming month. If they don't pay it, then you can take it out of their deposit and start an eviction process. Do not let the tenants get away with not taking care of their own repairs. I have added a sample repair sheet to the Appendix of this book.

Mistake 11: Failure to Inspect Regularly

You or your manager should visit your properties once a month. Pick a certain day of the week, notify the tenants, and make note of any repairs that need to be made. Have your manager give you a written report if you can't be there in person.

Even if you have a manager giving you written reports of the inspections, as an owner you still need to go inside your properties about every 90 days. If you happen to own properties outside of where you live, you need to travel to those areas to be able to go inside the properties themselves. You're playing a risky game if you do not inspect the properties yourself.

Establish one day per month to go in and check the smoke detectors and HVAC filters. Once inside, you are able to visually inspect the house and smell the smells, etc. One thing I learned early on is that by going in, you will notice if other people could be living in the house who are not listed on the lease. The tenants will need to have them leave, or you as the landlord can put a "no trespass" on those living in the property.

Mistake 12: Being Oblivious to Cycles

When supply is historically up—in other words, there are more houses on the market, the prices are flat, or they will be dipping some—that's the time to start looking for potential investment property.

If you want to wait a little longer, you have to pull the trigger a little quicker. When demand begins to absorb supply, which happens right after supply is at its peak, you can wait for supply to begin to edge down a little bit and demand to pick it up. When you see that prices may be trending up a little bit, that's also a time to buy. But you want to be always buying when there is more supply than demand.

To buy and flip, wait just a tad later in the cycle. Wait until demand begins to absorb the supply. Then start buying and flipping while the demand is increasing and before a lot of new construction begins.

Mistake 13: Being a Know-It-All

The next mistake is not having an experienced coach. When you have somebody coaching you, training you, teaching you, answering your questions, and helping you with challenges, it tremendously multiplies your chances for success. You will benefit greatly from a coach's experience and professional advice, so start looking for a coach now. You can also go to our website wealthbuilders .org for free and find an abundance of free blogs and vlogs. If you would like coaching, we offer a one-year program and would be glad to send you information about it. Again, just go to our website wealthbuilders.org.

You can also find coaches by going to real estate investors clubs, association meetings, or other gatherings where you would find like-minded people. Find somebody to model, someone who has built a business that you want to build. Most successful people are willing to give their advice for free, especially if you have some sort of connection. Again, it tremendously increases your chances for success if you invest the time to find a coach.

In addition to having experienced coaches, listen to CDs, watch DVDs, read books, go to seminars. Expose yourself to the market and keep up with the market on websites and resource sites.

Mistake 14: Not Having an Exit Strategy

The next mistake is not identifying your exit strategies. You must know what your long-term goals are. Whenever you buy and flip, remember that a good goal is to set a time frame for when you will get your money back.

You have to ask yourself if you will be able to sell the house in 90 days, 120 days, or maybe even six months. If you don't identify your exit strategies, you will not know how to put the deal together properly, and you will not know what to say no to. Knowing your exit strategy helps you understand what formula you're using and when and how you will get your money back.

Here are a couple of exit strategies. You can buy one house a year for 11 years. On the 12th year, refinance the first house you bought. In that time the house should have doubled in value. If you purchased the house for $100,000 and put $10,000 down 11 years earlier, during that time the amount that you paid on principal should have reduced the amount owed to around $75,000. The house has doubled and is now worth $200,000. You can easily get a refinance mortgage for 80% loan-to-value which is $160,000. The new loan pays off the amount owed which is $75,000 and the remaining amount $85,000 is paid to you the owner. You can now do whatever you wish with the total amount of that money. There are no taxes due since it came from a loan and not a sale. So you can live off of it or go buy a boat—whatever you want to do with it because it is not a taxable event. Then do the second house the next year, the third house the next year, and do it for 10 years. Every year you could be pulling approximately $60,000-$85,000 out per home to live off of tax-free because it's a cash-out refinance.

Another option is to buy three to 10 houses a year with a $300 positive cash flow per house and retire when you get to 30 houses. At this point, your cash flow will be about $100,000 a year tax-free. That is $300 per house times 30 houses equals $9,000 per month times 12 months equals $108,000 per year. By that time, you would have been approved by the IRS as full-time real estate professional and your write-offs would not be limited. The depreciation alone would more than likely cover all of the positive cash flow so you would not owe any taxes.

You could also buy three houses a year until you get to 20 houses, hold them for 11 years, sell 10, pay off the other 10, and live off the cash flow from the 10 that you just paid off. If the cash flow is $1,000 a month in rents per house, you'll have around $90,000-$100,000 a year.

Remember, that money will not be tax-free because you've now paid off the houses. When you've paid off the houses, you'll still have some depreciation left to protect you from taxes. I encourage you to think about it. These are great formulas for financial independence.

Whatever your exit strategy is, it should bring you to financial independence. You are building wealth.

Today, I've given you 14 mistakes that new investors should avoid making. As you avoid them, you should be able to develop your real estate business and knowledge more quickly and efficiently.

Since you purchased this book, and you've read this far, I'm going to give you seven bonus mistakes to avoid.

Bonus 1: Contingency Clauses

The first bonus mistake is not having contingency clauses in your contracts. Usually, everyone knows to always have a contingency on financing, but sometimes people want the pre-approval letter before they ever accept your contract. You want to be able to have some outs in the contracts that you write. Always make financing a contingency, which means if you don't have the financing by a certain period of time within the contract, then you're able to get out of the contract. Make having an inspection a contingency as well.

Also, if you are writing a number of contracts at one time, remember to include the contingency of your partner's approval. To operate with integrity, you should never write a contract that you don't intend to close on or have the capability to close on. However, having the partner contingency in a contract can cover a multitude of problems that can arise and cover your backside.

You can put many different kinds of contingencies in a particular contract, but these are the three main ones: financing, inspection, and approval of a partner.

Bonus Mistake 2: Overthinking

Another mistake that new investors make is overanalyzing deals and not pulling the trigger. As I've said several times, know your formulas and stick to them. If a particular property meets the formulas, then be willing to pull the trigger. Some people have become paralyzed trying to make deals.

If you know your formulas, then don't overanalyze! They either meet it or they don't. If you follow the pointers I have outlined in this book and you avoid making these mistakes, you've got a good deal.

Bonus 3: Bank Lines of Credit

A lot of times, investors will only use mortgage companies or mortgage broker shops to be able to finance their deals. It's important that you use bank lines of credit, especially to help you in deals that need to move quickly or deals that need major rehab.

Let me give you a nugget: just because one bank tells you they can't work with you does not mean the next bank will tell you the same thing. Not all banks are created equal, and not all banks are in the same position as the other banks. Sometimes you have to go to multiple banks before you find one that is in a position to work with you.

Of course, as I've said, you want to have some cash reserves and you need to be working on your credit score. If these things aren't perfect, don't be afraid to go in. Talk to the bank and show them your deal. It's a learning process.

Many times, on larger apartment buildings, they don't even look at your personal credit. They just look at the net operating income of the building and whether you have the experience to manage those kinds of properties. In some cases, they will just take the building where it is and you're able to buy it. Don't resist or avoid getting bank lines of credit. Go for it and establish those relationships!

Bonus Mistake 4: Prepaying the Contractor

Another mistake I see is paying contractors before they finish the rehab. Any final payment you give to contractors should be tied to whatever governmental inspection is necessary for that property to be ready to rent. Make sure you have clean agreements that spell out the final payment must be tied to inspections on the property. When that government agency has signed off on it and passed it for inspection, then you can pay your contractor.

Bonus Mistake 5: Pre-approval Letters

Another mistake I see is not obtaining a pre-approval letter from the buyer. You cannot afford to take your property off the market while you wait for approval, because if they aren't approved, then you've got to put it back on the market. Make sure that the buyer is pre-approved.

Always remember this: there is a difference between a pre-approval letter and a pre-qualification letter. You want a pre-approval letter because it has already been run in a mortgage system through what's called *automated underwriting.* Make sure the buyer has proof of funds and verifies if they're going to pay cash.

This filters out the less serious buyers. Always make sure that they give you a letter with the contract that they're submitting for your property for pre-approval.

Bonus Mistake 6: Failing to Prequalify a Tenant

You always want to get a credit check. You have to get approval from the tenant to pull their credit, but you can work with one of your mortgage brokers. Those credit checks will cost you anywhere from about $10-$20, which you will charge the tenant.

You also want to get a criminal check. Ask your local law enforcement to find out where to do that.

Here is a nugget: don't rent to somebody who doesn't allow you to see where they currently live. It's important to see where people currently live because that will tell you how they're taking care of the property. It's a whole lot easier to find a good tenant than it is to get rid of a bad tenant.

Lastly, there is a national tenant database that you can access to find out if there has been a problem with that particular tenant in other states. If you're using a management company, make sure the management company is properly prequalifying the tenants.

Bonus Mistake 7: Section 8 Evaluation

The great thing about Section 8 is that the rents are usually higher because there is typically a premium in most areas. They will pay $50 or, in some cases $100, higher than the going rents because HUD established what's called the *fair market rent values* for a particular area. You're able to see how much they'll pay for a one-bedroom, two-bedroom, three-bedroom, and four-bedroom property.

The other thing you have to remember about Section 8 is the government will pay most of the rent. The check actually comes directly from the public housing authority that is funded by HUD. The rents are guaranteed within that context.

Of course, you will have to put up with Section 8 inspections. About once every six months, they inspect the property and there are certain guidelines. You have to manage the tenants a little bit tighter than you normally would. You have to do the same screening on the tenants that you would on any open-market tenant because Section 8 does not prescreen them.

However, if they do violate the lease then they not only get removed from your property, but Section 8 will also kick them out so there is a double incentive for the tenants to do what's right.

CHAPTER 7

TOP 10 SECRETS OF REAL ESTATE FINANCING

The ability of the average consumer and investor to get loans dramatically changed in the early 1990s when the mortgage industry went to computerized lending. That birthed the credit score into existence and elevated its importance. Lending became difficult again during the Great Recession of 2008-2011 and began to get better beginning in 2012. In 2020, there remains a good number of loan products for the real estate investor.

Direct underwriting, the ability to get computerized underwriting instead of human attention, made underwriting loans fairly quick. The real estate market, in turn, became a whole lot more liquid than it was in the previous 100 years.

A lot of investors get hung up on the lack of knowledge when it comes to loans and how they work. Many people have talked about creative financing techniques, but the truth of the matter is, creative financing usually requires tighter property management and closer attention to cash flow by the investor to do a true, nothing-down deal.

You can work with individual sellers and arrange for creative financing in different ways, however, the quickest and the most efficient way to buy real estate is to have a good credit score and a little bit of cash to get started. In order to get a loan or to buy real estate, you have to understand how to get the financing that's necessary.

Now let's get into the top ten secrets that every investor should know about real estate loans.

Secret 1:
Know How Lending Markets Work

An investor needs to at least have a basic understanding about how the lending markets work. The first market I want to talk about is the retail lending market. This is when mortgage brokers and banks intersect with the retail buyer or retail investor as well as any home buyer that is looking to get a loan.

The lenders underwrite the loan according to certain criteria. Then, they take all of the loans they have originated and sell them to what's called the *secondary lending market*. It's important to understand that especially as an investor because those loans must meet certain underwriting guidelines in order to be sold.

Occasionally, you will find a lender that will hold loans within their portfolio which is called *portfolio lending*. Local banks will do this with you if you set up a good relationship.

The good news is there are so many loan products for the investor. As the markets began to change, more products were available online. This made the retail lending market easier for the investor because there were more loan products to meet the needs of an investor.

The secondary lending market is where the quasi-government mortgage banks and a large number of private sector mortgage banks purchase pools of loans that come from the retail lending market. They put them together and then repackage them in larger pools to sell to investors in the equities lending market.

So, we have the retail lending market, which is where investors primarily interface. The secondary lending market is where government agencies and some large private sector mortgage banks purchase these pools of loans. That's where pension funds, insurance companies, mutual funds, and foreign investments are purchased as packages of loans as mortgage securities, similar to stock. That's why we call it the *equities lending market.*

The key thing to know here is what keeps the mortgage lending industry liquid. In the foreseeable future, the lending market is going to be very liquid for real estate. Because of computerized lending, we now have three phases of the lending market: the retail lending market, the secondary lending market, and the equities lending market. The good news is that there are many investor products that are out there in this three-phase market in order for investors to get loans.

This is the golden age of the investor. This is the time that you should be buying real estate because the liquidity and the availability of funds is still out there, and I see it continuing to be that way for a long time.

Secret 2:
Mortgage Banker versus Mortgage Broker

The second secret is the difference between a mortgage banker and a mortgage broker. A mortgage banker usually sells his own products. The pros to this are that they typically can close faster and sometimes give the customer a low-interest rate or a lower cost. The cons are that the loan products they offer can be limited, which means sometimes they cannot get a loan done.

A good illustration for this would be Sears. Sears had all of its products with the Sears name brand on them, and that's what a mortgage banker does. In other words, a mortgage banker is someone who originates loans for larger banks. Sometimes there are actual bankers who have their warehouse line to work with.

Warehouse line means they basically have a lot of credit that they can use to be able to make loans, though there are lots of criteria that the loan must meet. The problem is that most of the time, investors can't meet those criteria.

Mortgage bankers are good because they can close quickly, but it's absolutely imperative that you understand their products are extremely limited. They could turn you down, but you could go across the street to a mortgage broker and they would give you four different products to choose from.

Mortgage brokers typically work in what we call a *broker shop*. The normal broker shop has less than 10 loan officers working for it. But a broker is exactly that—they broker loans. In most cases, they represent many lenders. An experienced, knowledgeable mortgage broker can meet or sometimes beat the offer of a mortgage banker as well as get the loan funded because they have so many lenders available.

Not all mortgage brokers are made equal. A lot of broker shops will only use two to three lenders from the secondary market to buy or fund their loans. This is because the more loans they do for an individual lender, the better deals they get as a broker shop. That being said, you need to find a mortgage broker who is experienced in working with investors.

If you become a fairly determined investor, you should have two or three mortgage brokers that work with you. Whenever you're making an offer on a property, make sure to have a pre-qualification letter, and in some cases, a pre-approval letter. Pre-qualification means the broker or the banker has run it through their underwriting program and, as long as your loan application looks good, they will give you a pre-qualification letter.

A pre-approval letter is when the processing officer and the loan officer go through your application, verify everything, and then run it through an underwriting program. Pre-approval gives you a little bit more weight when you're negotiating than pre-qualification, but in most cases, a pre-qualification letter is good enough.

Secret 3:
Purchase a Property for Less Than it Is Worth

The most important thing for you to know about real estate is that you make money when you buy, not when you sell. Your goal is to buy a property at the best possible price so when you sell it, you can make a higher profit margin, plus any equity if you held it for a while.

It is much more efficient if you have some of your own money to put up for a down payment. The power to negotiate with someone when you're purchasing a property is much greater when they know you have the money to buy it. You don't have to spend all of your time trying to come up with creative financing. You just go in, make the offer, negotiate on value, and try to get the best price you can for the property.

You want to always buy a property at a lower cost than what it's worth. I can tell you from experience that the safest way you grow your investment is to buy the property with cash and you're doing that through a loan. That's why it's so important to understand real estate finance, develop those relationships with a mortgage broker and a mortgage banker, and then understand how to keep your money moving.

The approach that I take in buying real estate is I want to be able to purchase the real estate at eighty cents on the dollar. That's 80% of the real value of the property, even after the repairs. The reason is that 20% equity in that property puts you in really good shape, and later if you want to refinance, you can.

It will be necessary to do what's referred to as an *investor purchase mortgage,* which means you'll have to have a down payment. What I recommend is that you buy your first several properties with 10% down if possible.

The point I want to make is that you're in a whole lot stronger position negotiating if you are able to bring a little money to the table. Also, most lenders want to see you have six-months cash reserves of the mortgage payments, which includes principal, interest, taxes, and insurance.

For example, if your mortgage payment is $1,000 a month, lenders like to see $6,000 liquid in the bank plus whatever the down payment is you've arranged. In this example situation, the down payment would be 10%. For a $100,000 house, you would need $10,000 for your down payment plus $6,000 in addition to that to show as six-month reserves. In your first several purchases, the additional cash beyond the down payment may not be necessary.

Secret 4:
How to Raise a Down Payment

How do you come up with that down payment? One of the greatest stagnant assets in America today is home equity. Your home equity is basically the value of the home minus the amount owed on any mortgages or liens. As you understand how to invest in real estate, you can pull money from the equity you have in your home. You can do this with a *cash out refinance loan* where an appraiser comes in to give you an appraisal on the new value of the home because it's appreciated over time. You can cash out the equity you have in your home, and then a bank will loan you 80-90% on the new value. You can use that money to begin investing in real estate.

Another way to raise a down payment is through retirement accounts. A lot of people don't know this, but you can now use your IRA or a simplified employee pension plan (SEP) to purchase a second home or to buy an investment property. In some cases, you can actually use a tax-deferred pension plan (Keogh plan). There are some criteria, but it is a good option to look into. Instead of using the money out of the retirement account to purchase real estate, you can also just borrow against your plan. Then you don't have as many restrictions.

You can raise money from your own liquid assets as well. You can use or borrow against the cash, stocks, bonds, insurance policies, etc., that you already have and use that for a down payment to get started in real estate.

My favorite way to raise a down payment is to use lines of credit from local banks. There are two lines of credits from the banks. One is a true line of credit where you can write a check for anything you want. You can go buy a pair of shoes or buy a house. I have used those for rehabbing properties quite often.

The second way to raise money is when a property is connected to what you're borrowing. The bank will give you the preapproval letter, but they have certain ratios. Typically, a bank will not loan more than 80% of the value of the house, and that includes rehab. That means if you paid $0.70 on the dollar for the property, the bank would loan you 100% of the 70%. Then you could use the

$0.10, which would take you up to $0.80 on the dollar. With an 80% loan-to-value, the bank would loan you that extra 10% in order to do the rehab. Some banks don't require you to put any of your own money in that deal. Don't be concerned about having to talk to a lot of banks. Look around for community-type banks and local banks. They typically loan to builders.

You can get lines of credit that are connected to the property itself, which gives you tremendous leverage in acquiring the property. Most of those loans last for six to 12 months. I get mine for 12 months, and then I refinance that loan when it starts coming out.

Because there is no seasoning requirement by local banks, you can refinance that loan in 60 days and get 100% of your money back in your pocket. Most properties that I have purchased with the banks, I refinance out in 60 to 90 days. I will put anywhere from $5,000 to $25,000 in my pocket and continue to make a positive cash flow on that property.

Again, the key is that you make money in real estate when you buy, not when you sell. If you bought the property at a low enough loan-to-value on the dollar, you can do that every time with a property. Lines of credit are one way to raise a down payment.

Another way to raise a down payment is credit cards. Obviously, I'm not a big fan of this, but I'll tell you about it anyway. You can get cash advances on your credit card, depending on what your interest rate is and the type card you have. This is not a really smart way to go unless you really understand how to invest in real estate. I've personally never done this, but I've known other investors who were wise enough to know how to work that plan. My opinion is if you spend enough time establishing relationships with local banks, you don't have to use your credit cards for cash advances.

Another way you can raise a down payment is with partners. I think a lot of real estate investors miss this one. Typically, this works with the partner putting up the money, and you putting the mortgage in your name. You bring the deal, you do the rehab, you set up the management if you're going to buy and hold, or you put the property up for sale with a realtor. Then, whenever the property is sold, you and your partner split the profits 50/50. It's an easier way to raise a down payment when you spend your time investing in real estate.

You can also get a down payment from the seller. This is creative, but it's not overly difficult. You can find sellers who are willing to carry back from 10-30% of the purchase price as a down payment. When a lender does a first mortgage on a house, that lender won't lend any more than 80%. They're willing to loan 80% on any home based on the purchase price as long as the appraisal backs up the purchase price. Sometimes they will do what is called a *desk review appraisal* where they actually look up the property through some different websites and check to see what the value of the property is.

As long as the appraisal is there, they will own 80%. As long as you can afford a *full doc loan* or a *stated loan*, you can find a lot of lenders who will lend you 80% on that. The seller likes that because they get back their money.

The good news is that if you put the loan in your name, in 12 to 36 months you can refinance it and take the seller out of it. The seller is happy, and you basically just purchased a property for no money down. So that's another way to find a down payment!

Secret 4: Know Your Credit Score

The mortgage market drastically changed for the good in the early 1990s for two reasons. The first reason is that it became computerized. The second reason is that the FICO credit score was invented, which enabled lenders to quickly and easily assess the risk of lending to investors. Many loans can get approved in just a few minutes. Very frankly, experienced loan officers or brokers know how to play with it so they can tell you quickly what to do if you aren't approved. The term *FICO* comes from "Fair, Isaac, and Company," named after the company who designed the model for our credit scoring. The model they use for the credit score is proprietary information, which is not made public. In other words, they don't tell you how they score.

A credit score that is 760 and above really is worth about $250,000 to you. The reason I say that is because as a real estate investor, you're able to have more products at each range. The highest score is in the 850 range. An outstanding score is the 760 score. In fact, 760 and up gets you the same interest rate as an 850 score. You are basically getting the same products. A good score is 680 and above. When you get down to 620, you're in danger. As a real estate investor, your goal is to have a credit score no lower than 660. If you're not at a 660, then I encourage you to take a year and work on your credit score.

Because of the changes that happened in the early 1990s, and again after 2012, the availability of investor loans become more prolific. You no longer have to spend all your time trying to creatively finance.

The best deals in real estate usually happen when you can pay cash for a property. You get the best value, your investment is more safely hedged, and you make more money.

You need to spend a lot of time getting yourself into a position to borrow money from mortgage lenders so you can walk in with some negotiating power to buy properties. I call it *value investing in real estate*. If you have a low credit score, start working on it! Then, at the same time you're working on your credit score, study and listen to real estate training courses. Begin looking at properties and gaining knowledge about real estate and the real estate market.

Even though the exact scoring of FICO isn't released to the public, we do generally know the five factors of credit scoring. Payment history accounts for 35% of the weighting of a credit score. If you have a low credit score, start paying your bills on time. Late paying kills a credit score.

Another thing that is weighing on your credit score is outstanding credit balances. You should never owe more than 50%. For example, if your credit limit is $10,000, then never owe more than $5,000 on that credit card. If you really want to keep it impeccable, then you should never owe more than a third or 33%. So, if you have a credit line of $10,000, you would never charge more than

$3,300. It doesn't build your credit to pay off the balance every month. What creditors want to see is that you're able to make your monthly payment. I encourage you to keep your balances down, and occasionally just pay the minimum payment on the card. That reflects very well on your payment history.

Outstanding credit balances is weighted at 30%. Credit card balances are weighted against you if they are too high. Mortgage debt does not weigh against you as badly as credit cards or installments, so you want to keep those credit balances down.

The length of your credit history is weighted as 15%. How long you've had credit is a critical thing because it shows lenders that you have experience paying down debt.

The number of inquiries make up 10% of the score. A lot of people get worried because if they're shopping for cars or things that require credit checks, they think it will decrease their score. I personally don't let people check my credit unnecessarily for a lot of reasons, but if it is necessary, don't worry about it affecting your overall score too much.

Now, let's consider how your FICO score affects your interest rate. Typically, the higher your credit score the lower your rate.

There are three credit bureaus: Experian, TransUnion, and Equifax. When a mortgage lender looks at your loan application and pulls your credit for review, they will consider scores from all three of the bureaus. Then, they will take the middle score from those three companies to determine what your credit score is. At the time of this writing, many lenders have their own exclusive credit score modeling that they use. However, the FICO score is still the standard.

Bankrate.com tells us that:

- 25% of all credit reports contain errors that may result in you being denied loans
- 79% of all credit reports contain mistakes of some kind
- 54% contain incorrect personal information, which can affect you as well
- 30% contain closed accounts listed as open.

To dispute errors on a credit report, you can do what's called a *mail-in dispute* in 30 to 45 days and try to get it resolved. You can typically do an online dispute, and they'll correct it within 30 days. If you've been denied credit, your lender can do what's called a *quick score* or *rush corrections* for you.

In order to get a credit report online, I recommend going to the individual websites of the three credit reporting agencies: www .Experian.com, www.TransUnion.com, and www.Equifax.com. Normally, it costs about $15, but you get the report and your score. Be sure to request both.

Do's and Don'ts During a Loan Process

Firstly, if you're applying for a loan, don't apply for new credit anywhere else. Secondly, you can pay off accounts, but **do not close them.** If you close them, it will lower the amount of credit limits, which will raise the ratio of the debt you owe to the credit limits that you have. You don't want to make a lot of changes while a lender is looking at your credit. Thirdly, don't max out or over-charge your cards. Keep them in that ratio that I recommended earlier (never more than 50% on each card). Fourthly, don't consolidate debt to one to two cards during the loan process. Lastly, don't raise red flags to the underwriters by cosigning on another loan or changing addresses. Believe it or not, moving during the period of the loan process actually will raise red flags.

During the loan process, do join a credit watch program. That's exactly what I just described for you. Make sure you stay current on all the accounts that you currently have. Go ahead and continue to use your credit as you have been doing. That obviously looks as though you're living your life and handling your finances normally.

Secret 5:
Know What Matters to an Underwriter

What actually is important to an underwriter? Well, we just went over credit scores and established that a 760 credit score and up is worth about $250,000. We call it the *$250,000 credit score*. It allows you to finance multiple properties.

One of the formulas I teach is to own 30 single family homes with at least a $300 positive cash flow per month after principal, interest, taxes, insurance, and management fee. You literally can get yourself into making $100,000 a year tax-free with that kind of setup. The point is that 760 score allows you to continue to buy multiple properties because it allows you to access the products that are in the mortgage industry. Of course, that credit score allows you to have greater flexibility.

The next thing an underwriter or an underwriting program would look at is your capacity. In other words, they look at what is called the *debt-to-income ratio*. Underwriters always factor in ratios, which displays your income capacity to repay the loan. The standard guideline is no more than 28% of your monthly gross income for your mortgage payment and no more than 36% of your gross monthly income for all debts including your mortgage payment. However, this is where the credit score comes in again. Many lenders allow higher debt ratios, especially if your credit score is good.

The first loan that investors could start with is what's called the *full doc loan* or a *full documentation loan*. On this particular loan, they will ask you for documents like your past two years of tax returns and your past two months' of pay stubs or checking account statements. They will also do a verification of employment (VOE) and or verification of your assets (VOA).

They're looking for "seasoned funds," which are the funds that would be used for your down payment and six months of mortgage payments. They want to see these funds "seasoned" or have been at that particular balance in your name for the past 60 days. Sometimes, they will do what's called an *average balance* to determine that the funds have been sitting there for at least 60 days.

After a real estate investor has purchased five to 10 properties in his or her name, it's wiser to go from a full doc loan to a stated income loan. If you're self-employed or a business owner, you may start off with a stated income loan. Let me explain how that works.

The loan is typically classified as a stated income/verified asset loan. A real estate investor will do this loan as they begin to accumulate more and more properties.

The self-employed and business owners receive a 1099 for their income. Most of the time, stated income is not accepted if you are not a business owner or self-employed. If you're a beginning investor, you need to be careful about how your income is stated.

If you're more sophisticated with multiple properties, lenders will allow you to state your income at whatever it needs to be so the debt-to-income ratio is satisfied based on all your debts. Again, this is only a possibility if you have a good credit score.

The third thing underwriters look at is collateral. They're looking at the property itself and what's called the *loan-to-value ratio (LTV)*. The loan-to-value ratio is determined by an appraisal.

Lenders who loan the first mortgage won't loan more than 80% loan-to-value on a property. If you go to 90% loan-to-value, they will require mortgage insurance on the property. What people don't realize is when you purchase mortgage insurance, you have to go through another underwriting program just like getting a second mortgage.

Many times, the cost of the mortgage insurance is more than just getting a second mortgage on the property, so the lender is able to do what's called an *80-10-10 loan*. They loan 80% on the first mortgage and 10% on the second mortgage, which is typically at a much higher rate than the first. You then put 10% down. It's called an *80-10-10 loan*. In other words, 80% first mortgage, 10% second mortgage that equals 90% LTV (loan-to-value). Then you put 10% down of your own funds. There are higher loan-to-value ratios. You can do a 95% loan that typically is done in an 80-15 type loan and then 5% of your own funds. That would be 80% on the first mortgage, 15% on the second LTV, and you put 5% yourself.

If your credit score is good, there are actually 100% loans in the private sector market available. For example, lenders will do a 75% first and a 25% second, or in some cases, they will do an 80% first and a 20% second for a 100% loan. You would pay a much higher interest rate on that second mortgage, but when you combine the two interest rates, you could be left with a pretty good cash flow.

The exciting thing about collateral on a loan itself is that if you purchase a property correctly, you can refinance in six to 12 months and get all of your money back, put money in your pocket, buy another property, and still collect cash flow on the previous property.

The next thing that underwriters look at is your character. For sure they will look at how long you've been on the job. For example, they want to see that a person has worked at least two years on your VOE. Underwriters also like to see you at the residence that you currently live in for at least two years. Occasionally, that can have an affect on their decision even if you're moving to a new home.

Underwriters also consider your age. Age 50 truly is better than age 30. So, for those of you who are in the baby boomer generation and feeling a little older, you actually have a leg up. That doesn't mean those of you who are 25 and 30 will be overly penalized, but they do take it into consideration.

Secret 6:
Know What Loan Products Are Available

The first type of loan I want to discuss are fixed-rate loans, which come in 30-year and 15-year intervals. If you do a fixed rate as a real estate investor, I strongly encourage you to do a 30-year fixed rate.

If you know you will only keep a property for five years or so, adjustable rate mortgages have what's called a *3-1 product*. It means that the interest rate is locked in for three years and is an adjustable rate. You will pay principal and interest on that three years. At the end of the three years, the interest rate can adjust every year thereafter connected to a particular index. There is a 5-1 loan where the interest rate is locked for five years, and then every year thereafter, it changes. Then there is a 10-1 adjustable rate mortgage where the rate is then fixed for 10 years. You need to compare these different interest rates to see which one is best for you.

There are also government loans and federal housing administration (FHA) loans. These are good especially for first-time home buyers who are required to put down only 3% of the purchase price. As an investor, government programs tend to have a difficult qualification process. This is the reason you need an experienced broker or loan officer on your team who knows all about the various loan products that are available.

Secret 7: Expect Turbulence

I fly on airplanes several times a month, and there's one thing about flying I've learned for sure. You can be riding along enjoying a smooth flight, when all the sudden, you run into severe turbulence. Likewise, you can encounter turbulence during the loan process, too.

Turbulence can happen if you don't tell the truth on your loan application. Let me give you a nugget: not all your indebtedness has to be against you personally; it can be against your business. This way, it doesn't report against you on a personal loan. When you do a bank loan, you need to report the business debt as well, because they will ask you for it even though it's not in your name. However, in a mortgage loan, you're not lying if you withhold that information because your business actually is 100% responsible. You're not personally responsible. However, you must always be 100% honest.

Turbulence can happen if you have a recent late payment on a credit report. That's why you need to be checking your credit report all the time and be watching any loans you have, to make sure they're paid. I cannot emphasize this point to you enough.

If the loan officer or the mortgage broker finds out about additional debt after the loan application, you could hit some serious turbulence. This is why you need to look at your credit report before you apply to make sure you understand what's on there. If you're an investor, sometimes it can be difficult to obtain verification of rent, so you need to have the signed leases that show what your income is on your properties.

Bankruptcy within the last seven years can also cause turbulence. That is not a good thing when you're trying to borrow money as an investor or even on a personal home loan application. This is a big one.

Turbulence can happen when a borrower changes jobs; it throws the whole process into a tailspin. That's why you don't want to change many things during the loan process. In our office, we've set up a system with my accountant and attorney so that we keep all the things that are critical consistent. It's important that you learn to be consistent in the process.

Another type of turbulence is if a buyer comes up short of money at closing. You need to make sure you have those liquid funds. Turbulence can happen if you do not own 100% of the property as previously disclosed.

Another turbulent situation is not completing the repairs that were agreed to in the contract. That can hold the closing up and, in some cases, stop it all together. Sometimes, an escrow company fails to obtain information from beneficiaries or lien holders, insurance companies, or lenders in a timely manner. I've personally experienced that, and it holds up the closing.

Sometimes an appraiser will make a mistake on the appraisal and bring the value in too low. That will hold it up as well.

There are over 100 turbulent situations, and here I just listed a few. The point is to expect things to go wrong and know how to fix them.

Secret 8:
Negotiate the Cost of a Loan

A good rule of thumb is the closing costs should be well less than 1% of the loan. You also want to look at what's called your *good faith estimate* or the *settlement statement.* That's the list of all the costs to the buyer and seller. On there, you want to look for junk fees like administration fees, doc prep fees, etc.

A mortgage broker may make 1% of the loan from you if you're doing one loan at a time. In my opinion, that is the maximum amount. Many loans have an origination fee that goes directly to the broker shop, and then they do a commission split with their loan officer. That origination fee should be no more than 1% unless the broker is not making anything on the backside of the loan, which is called a *yield spread.*

Secret 9:
Purchase Mortgage vs. Refinance Mortgage

It is extremely important to know the difference between a purchase mortgage and a refinance mortgage. When you do a purchase mortgage, you purchase a property in which you need a down payment. On a refinance mortgage, the property must have been in your name for the past six to 12 months. It's called *seasoning.* The good thing about a refinance loan is that you can get cash out.

Refinancing replaces the debt of one loan with another under possibly better terms. If you refinance, you might be able to get a better interest rate, but this type of deal isn't for everyone.

Secret 10: Manage Your Credit Score

I cannot tell you enough how important your credit score is. Again, you need to keep your credit card balances no more than 50% of available credit, and the best case is no more than a third of whatever your available credit is.

When you refinance, your credit can take a hit. Once you refinance one property, you want to make about 90 days of payments before you try to refinance another property or a group of properties. If you refinance several properties at a time, your credit score can take a 20-point hit even if you're doing everything right. Allow three months of mortgage payments, and that 20 points will come back up. Then, you can go refinance another property.

If you are a serious investor, form a corporation and have your autos and lines of credit put in the corporation's name without a personal guarantee. You can also do lines of credit after you've established a reputation and put it in the corporation's name. These loans will not reflect on your credit report because you do not personally owe them money. This is part of why the government has allowed us to establish companies. In these processes, your company acts as a third person for liability and debt reasons.

Therefore, you're able to get loans, and it doesn't show up on your credit report. That's a way to manage your credit report long term.

PART THREE

CHAPTER 8

| SECTION 8 HOUSING

Section 8 Housing refers to a property that is open to rent for clients within HUD. The purpose of Section 8 is to provide housing to low-income families. Primarily, they do that through what's called *rental assistance,* where the government actually pays for all or the majority of the rent.

Housing Vouchers

The way it works is the potential tenant will receive a housing voucher, usually based on an approval for the number of bedrooms. The particular housing voucher is good for about 60 days. That tenant has to go out into the open rental market and find a property.

As a landlord, the first thing to ask when someone says they're on Section 8 is for that housing voucher. That voucher will tell the prospective landlord how many bedrooms the person is approved for, and thereby, give the landlord an idea of how much rent will be paid by the housing authority for that tenant.

What we call the *Section 8 housing* is located in a public housing authority, which means the administration of the housing vouchers are all local. Let me explain how that works. A municipality or a county can set up a public housing authority (PHA) if they meet the guidelines. When they set that housing authority up, they have to meet HUD's guidelines. After it is set up, a government entity of that municipality will oversee it.

In Virginia, the city council oversees it, and in other areas the county commissioners oversee it. I see the same thing in Texas, Utah, and in other states. My home state is Colorado, and there we have housing authorities that are administered by the cities. It's important you understand how the system is set up, because depending on where you are, you can have a good experience or a bad one.

One of the reasons I like Section 8 is because if you're in a good housing authority, typically you will receive a premium in rents over and above what the open market rents are. In my opinion, Section 8 housing is a good way to go for someone who wants to buy and hold real estate to receive a positive cash flow. I will tell you that in Section 8, your properties do have to be managed a little more tightly and more often.

Advantages of Section 8

There are many advantages to renting Section 8. Firstly, the government pays the rent. This means your rent is guaranteed at the beginning of every month. You never have to worry that the check won't come.

Secondly, there will always be a steady stream of tenants. Tenants are always looking for properties, and Section 8 helps the tenants connect with your particular properties.

Thirdly, tenants are typically longer term than normal tenants. I have some tenants who have been in my properties for five or more years. This helps you because you won't have any vacancies. Those long-term tenants do a better job of taking care of the property, so my rehab and repairs are typically a lot less.

Fourthly, there is typically less competition with other investors because they tend to be scared of Section 8.

Fifthly, there can also be some reimbursement for any kind of tenant damage. That's an advantage of course since the housing authority itself is actually funding the particular cost of those damages.

Should I Rent Section 8?

Here is some important information you need to know about Section 8 to help you decide whether you will rent to Section 8. This first one is a real nugget, especially if you're new to the program. Rent is determined by what HUD calls the *fair market rent.* There is a fair market rent index for different areas, and one of the best ways to find it is on the www.HUD.gov website.

Though there can be quite a few housing authorities in one metro area, HUD will specify what the authorities will pay. Most of the time, utilities will be included in the fair market rent, so you have to subtract what the normal utilities would be.

I recommend you find what the price of houses are in your area and how much they've appreciated. You can do just some basic research on the Office of Housing Enterprise and Oversight, or you can use websites like www.Realtor.com. Then, check the fair market rents to see what they're paying for rents in Section 8.

You're looking for a 1-1.5% monthly return on the cost of your property, the same as the formula I taught for non-Section 8 housing. For example, if you bought a property for $50,000, you're looking for that property to rent for $500-$750 a month minimum, which lets you know that particular market is a good value play. The fair market rents will tell you if you should open your rents to Section 8.

You also need to understand HUD guidelines. One of the most important ones is that your property has to have one bedroom for every two occupants. It can be an apartment, it can be a duplex, it can be a single-family home, it can even be a mobile home, but it needs to have a bedroom for every two occupants.

I strongly encourage you to not buy any less than three bedrooms for a single-family home. For apartments, my personal opinion is that you don't buy less than two bedrooms, and the same with duplexes. Some people have done well in Section 8 housing with one-bedrooms, but my preference for appreciation and long-term value on any kind of property or unit is no less than two bedrooms. The largest portion of Section 8 tenants is single mothers who have children, which is why having at least two bedrooms is important.

HUD requires the landlord to sign a lease with the tenant, and they have to sign a housing authority contract called a *HAP* contract with the housing authority. The good news is that these are your (the landlord's) contracts. They are not HUD's contract. As the landlord, you can dictate what the tenant's responsibilities are. The housing authority will do frequent inspections to make sure that you, as a landlord, are keeping your property in good condition.

The landlord does sign a lease and a HAP contract that goes with the housing authority. It basically states what your relationship with the housing authority is. There is not a lot of paperwork, and you will begin to develop a relationship with the housing authority. The paperwork is no more than what you would do in a normal rental transaction with a tenant.

Screening Tenants

As the landlord, it's important that you screen the tenants just like any other tenant agreement. Just because a person comes to you with the Section 8 voucher does not mean they have been screened as tenants. It means they have been approved in the Section 8 housing program.

Let me tell you why this is so important. With Section 8 tenants you definitely need to do a criminal background check. Typically, you can use local law enforcement to run background checks. You also should do a credit check. One of the easiest ways to do a credit check is to use one of the local mortgage brokers. I get approval from the tenant when they sign that they will pay for the credit check on the loan application, and then I use a local broker to pull the actual credit check. A lot of times with Section 8, the prospective tenants have poor credit.

The credit check isn't as important as it would be for normal tenants because the housing authority is paying most of the rent, but it is still important to know.

Whenever you are screening a tenant for rent, one of the secrets is to go see where they live at that time. It allows you to see how they have taken care of the property they're in presently, and you can make taking care of the property a condition in the rental agreement. I don't rent to out-of-state Section 8 tenants or tenants who have lived in hotels/motels because you can't assess how well they take care of their living spaces. Don't tell them that, you just don't accept them as a tenant. You take the applications and then go with what you consider to be your best applicant for that property. This will prevent many headaches for you.

The tenants will never pay more than 30% of their income. Typically, tenants pay a maximum of $200 per month.

Inspections

Another thing to know is that inspections are done every 12 months. Let me give you some guidelines regarding inspections. Section 8s must have a separate living area, kitchen, bathroom, and one bedroom for every two persons. The living room and bedrooms must have two working outlets. The cover plates cannot be cracked or broken on the electrical outlets. All lights must have the actual covers on them. (I never figured out how tenants do this, but they seem to break those particular glass covers all the time. It's amazing.) There cannot be just a light bulb for lighting. All units must have a fire alarm and a smoke detector in working condition on each level. If you own a two-story house, there must be two of them. They check the batteries. All windows must be operational. They must be able to go up, stay up, and come back down. They have to be locked, and all windows must have screens. All entrances to crawl spaces, whether under the house, on the second floor, or going up into the attic, need to be covered. All steps, interior and exterior that are four or more steps, must have handrails, sometimes on both sides.

I've had properties where those rails were torn down, and the housing authority had us put them back in. Repairs that are necessary because of tenant damages are charged as rent due the next month, which the tenant must pay. This is why systems are important, and you must keep proper records. In some cases, where tenants have not paid for repairs over a period of time, you can use your records to replace your tenant with one who will take care of the property.

You must apply 60 days prior to the contract anniversary date for a rental increase. If your tenant moved in on July 1st of the previous year, you must apply for a rental increase by May 1st, at least 60 days prior.

In most cases, you'll get a $25-$50 per month increase. It's not always automatically approved. In fact, one of the insights I'll give you is that if a housing authority is being audited by HUD, they typically will not give you any increases in rent. You then have a choice: you can either take your property out of Section 8 and put it on the open market for higher rents or wait until they're willing to raise/meet your request for rent.

You can request whatever increase in rent you want. We had a property we were renting at the fair market rate. We requested $150 increase the next anniversary because property values had gone up, and they approved it. This increased our cash flow tremendously.

The housing authority's portion of rent is always mailed the first working day of each month and sent via snail mail.

However, as the landlord, you are responsible for the collection of the tenant's portion of the rent. Section 8 doesn't collect it for you.

If the tenants do not pay their portion of rent, you can report them to Section 8, and they will potentially kick them out of the program, not just out of your property. That's a powerful leverage for the tenant to pay their rent.

How to Get Your Property Listed

In order to get your property on the Section 8 list, call or visit the local housing authority and ask to have your properties put on it. In most cases, they'll post your property on the bulletin board or they'll actually hand the list to a prospective tenant who has been approved for a housing voucher.

With today's technology, you can list a property with online property management software on turbotenant.com or cozy.com and many others. The many sites that your property listing goes to for free will draw as many Section 8 tenants as you want. These types of cloud-based software are also good for running credit and criminal checks as well as receiving rent online.

You can also advertise your property online or in the local newspaper and put in that ad "Section 8 accepted." Potential tenants with vouchers will call you, you will interview them, take an application from them just like you would a normal tenant, run the criminal history check, and run the credit check. Before you go see where they live, contact the housing authority, and tell them what you're doing. They will get an inspection scheduled. The Section 8 inspector will inspect the property for the quality standards. They'll either sign off on it, or you will have to do some repairs, but then you will get the tenant in the property. You'll sign that HAP contract with the housing authority and begin to receive your rents.

I am a firm believer in Section 8 housing because you're able to receive premium rents as there is a shortage in Section 8 properties. In fact, the federal government has determined that the actual supply of low-to-moderate income housing for people who would qualify in Section 8 is diminishing by 50,000 units annually. You know what that means? That means demand for Section 8 housing is continuing to go up.

I strongly encourage you to look at Section 8 as a serious way to increase your cash flow on your rents.

CHAPTER 9

HOW TO PROFIT BIG BUYING VACATION PROPERTIES

Vacation properties can be a great investment if you have the financial capacity to purchase one. It can increase your net worth through appreciation and create a strong return with rental income. As I've said before, I like low-to-moderate income properties, but vacation properties that are well located can produce a tremendous return on investment.

My wife and I began to scout areas for vacation properties even though the majority of our portfolio is in low-to-moderate income housing. We found that there were some areas that were popular and in high demand, but the prices were depressed primarily because the economy was suffering.

I began to watch the price and the supply side of several areas, and I noticed the supply began to increase. As supply goes up, price begins to go down. As I was watching the behavior of the market, I noticed that the supply began to flatten out. I made sure this trend wasn't just during the high buying season, and I compared the same times in previous years.

I was already familiar with the area, so as I saw the supply drop, I began to look for properties. I wrote several contracts, and as we like to share, we wanted to buy property for $0.80 on the dollar. Always do this when you can! When it comes to luxury properties, you want to buy them close to their tax assessed value.

The property we bought was a very nice luxury property in great condition. It needed absolutely no work done. One of the keys to real estate is understanding the situation of the seller. This is even paramount over location when it comes to establishing a value play in real estate because the seller will determine what the value of that property is. In this situation, the seller was flexible because he was purchasing another vacation property on the East Coast and needed to sell the property to get his money out.

I made an offer that was 20% below the tax assessed value. We negotiated back and forth, and I ended up buying that property for about 17% below the tax assessed value at the current time, which was an incredible buy. I sold that property 12 months later and made approximately $100,000 in profit. Of course, I waited for 12 months to sell in order to avoid the earned income tax that you make if you flip properties within a 12-month period. All I had to pay was a capital gains tax.

If you're prepared to look at vacation properties and hold them for a 10 to 15-year cycle, you have the potential to make a lot of money. You have to buy the property correctly, though. The reason I like to use that time frame is playing the shorter game of buying properties is a little bit riskier.

Facts Regarding Vacation Properties

Vacation homes, on average, appreciate faster than other single-family homes. According to hotelcondo.com there are 5.1 million second homes currently in the United States. That demand will come primarily from the 79 million baby boomers and their children. Actually, we call them the *echo boomers* who are looking for second homes as well.

Approximately 60% of all second homes are purchased for recreational use. The other 40% is primarily investment property. Many second-home buyers will actually pay more for their second home than they did for their primary residence. In some cases, buyers will pay more for their second home than what their current primary residence is worth.

Most vacation properties are located less than 200 miles from the owner's residence.

Advantages of Owning Vacation Properties

One of my favorite advantages to owning vacation properties is what I call *short-term rentals.* These are people who will rent the property for a weekend or during the high vacation season, which is typically from December through March. You can find management companies that will handle everything so it can be hands-off for you. My goal is to only rent it part of the year, during the vacation season. I'm using the property the rest of the year basically for no cost. The folks who are renting that property are paying that property down while I'm enjoying the appreciation and use of the property.

Another advantage is what I call *substitution*. When you take a vacation somewhere, the cost can get pretty high. Take the amount of money you would have spent on a vacation and allow that amount of money to help you purchase a vacation property. You will create value when you're done with the vacation, and you'll have an asset to produce extra income. You can have a great time at your own vacation property with your family and create years of traditions.

Another advantage is the capital gains exclusion. If the home is considered a second home at the time you sell it, you can use it as a part of your retirement portfolio. Let me explain. If it is considered a second home, you must live in that home two of the previous five years before you sell it. You actually can make up to $500,000 as a married couple tax-free on that property. All of those years you get the tax advantages, you get the enjoyment, there was low maintenance, low headache, you were able to substitute your vacation dollars, and the government still allows you to pocket $500,000 tax-free.

The above scenario only works if you have claimed the property as a second home for two years out of the last five years on your taxes. The other three years it can be considered a rental property. For example, you could purchase a second home 10 years prior to your retirement and rent it out for eight years to receive the income and the tax benefits. Then the last two years before you retire, rent it out for no more than two weeks annually. The benefit of doing this means that you can then sell it, and the profits made on it up to $500,000 for a couple are tax-free. Yes, tax-free—not just tax deferred!

People will pay a strong five-figure a year income tax bill and never consider how a vacation property could help lower their taxes. If you're in a 25% tax bracket and you purchase that $300,000 property, you would save around $6,000 to $6,500 dollars a year just off of your taxes alone. That would help you toward purchasing the property.

Also, one of the biggest advantages of vacation properties is leverage. If you put $10,000 in the stock market, it would buy $10,000 in assets. If you receive a 10% return on that investment annualized, that's a $10,000 return that you made on your $10,000 investment.

If you purchase real estate, you can actually take the same $10,000 in cash, and instead of purchasing $10,000 in stock, you can purchase $100,000 in real estate because you would have 10% down. A lender will loan you the other 90%. Here's an example. Let's say you now have a $90,000 loan on the property. If that property appreciates 10%, you would get a $10,000 return on $100,000. This gives you a 100% return on the $10,000 that you put in. Additionally, you will receive cash flow, which would ideally be $1000 a month on this example property. That's $12,000 a year on one property. This would enable you to make your payments and escrow costs on the mortgage.

Appreciation is a huge advantage, especially in real estate. If you have a property that is worth $300,000, and it appreciates 6% in a year (which has been the average for the past 40 years), that's an $18,000 return on that $300,000 property.

Another advantage of vacation property is the equity builds up. If you do a fixed-rate loan every time that you make a payment, you're actually paying down the principal you owe on that particular property.

Another tremendous advantage of owning vacation property is you get to control the asset. When you purchase stock in the stock market, you have no control over whether that stock goes up or down. You do have control over when you buy and sell it, but you have no control over what actually happens to the stock itself. In real estate, you can control how you market the property to increase the return. You also can improve the property. You can put in new carpet, countertops, cabinets, or fix up the bathrooms. You can create value. You get to control when you rent it. You get to control when you use it, and you control when you sell it.

I also like vacation properties because they can be insured from loss. You can't insure from loss with stocks. I had fires in several of my properties over a course of years, and in both cases, I came out good because I always carry good insurance. Make sure you're over-insured.

The advantages of owning vacation property are incredibly powerful, and they're a very strong investment.

Determine Your Formula

Your goal is to purchase a property where you're able to rent it out during the peak vacation seasons. Let's say, for example, your peak vacation season lasts for 12 weeks (Memorial Day to Labor Day).

Ideally, you would want to have rented your property every week during that peak season. Remember, if you rent it for more than 14 days, it must be classified as an investment property.

The advantage of that is you get all the other deductions and benefits that an investment property brings with it such as depreciation, your travel to look at the property, and other deductibles. Driving or flying out to see your property and check on it while you stay in it, that's all deductible because you're using it as an investment property.

That 12-16 weeks you're renting it out should pay for the entire year. As a general rule, one week per month of payments. When I rent the property, I want to be able to make the one week for each month I have a payment. If I rent it for 12 weeks during the peak season, that gives me 12 monthly payments.

With your rent, you want to cover what I call *PITIM*, which is principal, interest, taxes, insurance, and your management fee. You should allow a total cost of about 10% for management and other costs if you rent your property through some of the popular internet sites.

Companies like Airbnb and VRBO.com make renting vacation properties easier than ever before. Because of these popular websites, you're able to pay less than you would by using a management company. It doesn't cause a big headache, especially if you have a local management company handling your keys, cleaning, and maintenance. You rent it, and they manage it. It's a powerful combination that allows you to pay for your vacation properties with the rental money that comes in.

Location, Location, Location

Plenty of people ask what areas they should target for vacation properties. There are ski areas, ocean areas, and all kinds of different places you could target. You need to always look at where supply is increasing. Many people are trying to get into the hot markets. If you can get into a hot market early enough, then I would say go for it. To protect yourself, unless you have other inside information, I'm always looking where supply has been increasing. An easy way to tell if supply is increasing is if there are an increasing amount of homes for sale in the area.

You have to research and watch for that in markets. You should contact a real estate agent in a particular area and ask if they could send you information on what the supply has been. This will typically be the number of properties that were on the market for the past three years. Then, ask them what the median selling price was in that area. You want to buy when supply starts going down a little bit and prices are still depressed somewhat. Typically, it's too late to buy in an area where heavy new construction has begun because that means that the market has already absorbed what's going on.

If you don't want to rent your property for 12-16 weeks, you still have a value play. You should purchase a property at $0.80 on the dollar. To do this, you can use the substitution method I mentioned earlier. Instead of taking an expensive vacation, use that money to buy a vacation property. You can also take your IRA and purchase a property.

You can classify a property as a second home when you purchase it if you're getting a loan on it. Then, you have every legal right to reclassify it as a vacation property when tax season comes around if you decide to rent that property for the 12-16 weeks. That way, you get all the tax benefits, and you're able to rent it for however many weeks you choose.

If you decide you want to hold this property for a while, you can live in it. While you're living in it, you will classify it again as a second home. You can't rent it for the 12-16 weeks. But if you have lived in it for at least 2 years as your primary residence, as stated earlier, you can sell that property with all of its appreciation and receive all the capital gains up to $500,000 tax-free.

Questions

By asking yourself a series of questions, you can determine what you're looking for when it comes to a vacation property. Here are several questions to help you define your search.

Ask yourself, "What are my reasons for wanting a second home?" My wife and I did this particular exercise several times. Honestly, we wanted a good quality, quiet place that we could get away to, as well as a place where we could take our children and grandchildren for them to really enjoy. Our answers to that one question led us to look for something that was fairly accessible to where we already lived.

One of the big questions to ask yourself is about size. In our case, we wanted something large enough to enjoy as a family, especially when it came to cooking a turkey at Thanksgiving. We knew our grandchildren wanted a swimming pool, and we knew our adult children wanted easy access to skiing.

Also ask yourself financial questions like, "How does this fit into my personal financial portfolio?" Frankly, vacation properties that are selected correctly can offer a better return long term than the stock market. I think you should seriously consider looking at vacation properties for just that reason. If you have help finding vacation properties, such as an accountant, lawyer, or real estate agent, ask plenty of questions. Ask if you should classify it as a second home or investment property. Ask about everything you've read in this book.

You also need to ask yourself what type of locations you are the most interested in. I looked at a great value play in a particular state where they were building a massive condominium-type complex with tremendous amenities. It was very good pricing at the time, and they were located on a bay. Are you interested in sitting on your deck and watching the seagulls go by? Are you interested in having a dock for your boat and the fresh breeze flow throughout your house? Or are you interested in snowy mountain towns with perfect skiing locations?

Research into the markets with the greatest future potential for appreciation is incredibly important. You want to see the supply of vacation homes, which you can check with a local realtor. You're also looking for something to tell you that either people are moving into the area, or outside folk will be interested in buying. One of the things that tells me about future potential is when prices begin to pick up. Another way you can look at price appreciation is to google the Office of Housing Enterprise and Oversight. It will give you what the appreciation has been over the last quarter and breaks that down into smaller communities and counties.

Remember, they are not making any more land on the ocean, and they're not approving very many more ski areas. This is important because that particular type of property is not being created. If it's a well-located ski area and the property is a good deal, you can know that the property values definitely will go back up.

Ask yourself, "What kind of loan would meet my needs the best?" As I've said, you want to make sure you get a preapproval for your loans. Then look at whether or not you want an interest-only loan or a fixed-rate loan. This will help you determine exactly what your payments will be.

Ask yourself about the price parameters of a potential property. I told you the formula for buying 80 to 90 cents on the dollar, but you want to compare the price per square foot, especially with vacation properties. If you're buying in a resort or vacation area, you'll have a large number of properties to compare.

You're looking to purchase the property at 80 to 90 cents on the dollar based on the sales comparisons in an area. Occasionally, you will find an outstanding located view property. Be careful not to overpay, but you can pay more for those properties because it will produce a great return when it comes time to sell. So, you ask yourself, "What is my price range? What can I afford?"

Make sure that you've looked at enough properties. Do not fall in love with the first property you find. Make sure you examine properties and look at them so you get a feel for the neighborhood.

What Drives Demand?

First of all, there are limited quality choices. For example, I enjoy skiing properties very much. One of the things I have learned is that the U.S. Forest Service will not issue any other permits for ski areas to be built in the United States. There may be a few here and there, but not many. Therefore, the properties and buildings located immediately around those ski areas, especially those with ski views, in walking distance to ski lifts or a short bus ride away, will be considered a limited quality choice. Waterfront properties are another good example of this. We cannot make any more ocean, so there are no more beachfront properties being made.

For the foreseeable future, there are low-interest rates in the mortgage industry. Interest rates are lower than they have been in years, and even for the next decade or so, it appears they will remain low. The opportunity to get financing that allows someone to own property at a reasonable rate per month because of low-interest rates creates demand, and it makes real estate a good investment.

The 73 million baby boomers are also creating demand, especially because they're looking for retirement homes. Many baby boomers today are using the home equity that is locked up in their primary homes and doing cash-out refinance loans.

They could do a second mortgage, a home equity line of credit, or refinance the entire property with a new first mortgage. They use the equity they pull out of their property to purchase a vacation home.

There is also a European demand. I was in Australia recently standing in line to board an airplane, and I started talking to other passengers to pass the time. They began to talk about the real estate in America, and in the process, they had mentioned a couple of locations they and their friends had purchased.

Demand has increased because supply has diminished. People are living longer and occupying their second homes longer. I like to use the illustration that there are only so many positions on a professional baseball team. In the same way, there are only so many well-located properties in the vacation market.

Technology also drives demand because it gives people the ability to be in a vacation location and still be productive. Demand for these types of properties is continuing to grow. That's why I want to teach you how to invest in vacation properties and what to look for when searching for the right deal.

How to Obtain Financing

After you understand demand, you need to obtain financing before you write any contracts to purchase properties. I encourage you to first obtain a preapproval letter before you look at properties because it gives you the leverage.

When you're buying vacation properties, always remember the less you put down, the better return you will receive, although your monthly payment will be higher. Most lenders require you to put 20% down, but some lenders will loan 90%, which I talked about earlier in the book.

A pre-qualification letter is typically all you need when you submit a contract, and then you have a certain number of days to get a commitment from your lender. If you write a contract, you close in 45 days. Of course, one of the contingencies in your contract is to get the financing. On your loan application, if it is appropriate for you, classify the property as a second home and not an investment property. This will get you better terms on your loan.

It is also incredibly important to know your credit score. In an earlier chapter, we talked about the importance of a credit score being 760. We call it *The $250,000 Credit Score* because it gives you so much flexibility. To be looking at a vacation property, you want your credit score to be at least 660 and up. I encourage you to purchase a credit report, not a free online one. Most of the time, the free ones do not actually give you the number of your credit score, or they aren't accurate. For $15 you can purchase from the credit bureaus Experian, Equifax, and TransUnion. It will cost you $45 for all three, it lets you know exactly where you are, and it does not "hit your credit" when you're purchasing it for yourself.

It's also important to have seasoned funds because the lender wants to see what is in the bank account. They will check what is in your name, not in your company's name, or a retirement account. Retirement accounts are fine, but lenders will only allow you to use 75% of the value of the retirement account as cash reserves. A lender wants to see you be able to put 10-20% down as seasoned money for 60 days. They also like to see three to six months of mortgage payments and liquid assets in some type of account. Again, if it's in a retirement account, they will only allow 75%.

Calculate Your Return

In order to calculate your return on an investment property, include your tax bracket, depreciation, and any positive cash flow. For a $300,000 investment property, take the total return and list appreciation. Residential real estate has appreciated historically at 6% so, for $300,000, the return would be $18,000 for the year. I encourage you to go to wealthbuilders.org and use the free real estate calculator to determine your total return.

Based on the formula I give you in this book, you can get as high as a $300 a month in positive cash flow on the $300,000 property, after all expenses. Then, you are allowed to take an investment property interest and depreciation. If you're in a 25% tax bracket on a $300,000 property, that comes up to $6,250. If you add all three of those numbers up—appreciation, positive cash flow income, and interest and depreciation expenses—you come up with a return of about $27,850 on a $300,000 property.

If you were to put $30,000 down to purchase the property, which would be 10%, the cash-on-cash return is almost 100%.

As stated earlier, when you consider your house a second home, you can only rent it for 14 days a year. However, the IRS doesn't require you to show that rental income anywhere on your taxes. You also get to deduct it off the interest you pay. However, you do not receive any depreciation on the property because it's considered a second home. If you were to do the total return and classify it as a second home, then you would take the appreciation again at 6% and receive $18,000 calculated in your return. There would be no income except for what you were able to rent for the 14 days.

So, let's just say you were able to make $2,500 on that property. You would add that in as well. Then you're able to deduct your interest. If you're in a 25% tax bracket, again the interest on that property comes out to a little over $6,000. Your return again—and these are just round numbers—would be close to $25,000. If you put $30,000 down, that's a very good cash-on-cash return as a second property.

Managing Vacation Properties

Vacation properties give investors a profit center for themselves, especially as they hold the property for longer periods of time. However, there are some secrets to managing a vacation property correctly.

The easiest way to manage a vacation property is to hire a management company. As I've said, it's almost exactly like purchasing stock on the internet in that you literally just hand the keys over to a management company in a particular area. They handle everything—the management fee, the renting of the property, the late-night plumbing calls. Your management fee will usually run from as low as 10% on a vacation property to as high as 50%. This is a good way to go for high-income individuals or people who are just looking for some tax relief.

The second way is actually my favorite. You don't quite get the maximum profit out of it, but you rent it yourself. You post your rental on some of the internet rental sites, which will cost money, but it gives your property tremendous exposure.

My favorite is www.VRBO.com, which stands for vacation rental by owner. Some of my other favorites are www.airbnb.com, www.CyberRentals.com, www.BeachHouse.com, www.VacationRental.com, www.AllRentalsByOwner.com, and www.HomeAway.com. You can post your vacation property on all these places.

Then, contract a management company so they handle the keys, cleaning, repairs, and any emergencies. The point is that the renters' personal experience is fantastic. They pick their keys up at the property, and they communicate with the management company. But we rent it through one of the internet websites, and that's also how we get paid.

My favorite part about renting these properties out myself is that it allows me to directly control who rents the property. This would not happen if the management company was renting the property. It also allows me to control vacancies across the board. If things slow down, I can do a little more advertising or use some other methods to get my property out there. I also control the vacancies or control the use of the property for myself, my family, and my friends. So, through personal experience, I prefer to rent properties out myself. I rent them through these websites, and I contract a management company to handle all the details.

The third way to manage a property is to not work with a management company at all. This means you would have to rent and manage the property yourself. I personally do not like this method. However, if you are close by or you want to take the time and energy to employ a good cleaning and repair crew, it's an option.

As I said before, an advantage to not working with a management company is that you can control the vacancies. I had a situation where I had a property that was rented and managed by a company. There was a season when I should have been receiving calls, but I found out that my property had been put in a rotation. Demand went down, and I lost six weeks of good rentals I should have had. For maximum income, you can rent it and manage it yourself, but it does take more time.

Written Rental Policies

Rental policies need to be posted on the website, especially the key ones, and they need to be sent in an email to renters. Since I personally rent our properties through websites, the policies we consider most important are actually posted on the website itself.

For example, we don't allow pets in our vacation properties. You can increase your profits by accepting pets because you will get a larger deposit, but the risk of damage is greater. We also enforce a nonsmoking policy. We do not rent to anyone under the age of 25 in order to avoid the college party situations. So, put in writing the policies that are important to you and post them. It's important!

Legal Setup

In order to maximize profits, you should accept credit cards. This seems intuitive, but it can be more difficult than it seems. I suggest you set up a merchant account in a business name to accept MasterCard and Visa. You can set up PayPal for checks, American Express, and Discover cards. This gives people a level of comfort because it's easy to pay, and they can get their money back if they don't end up renting your property.

When you accept credit cards, think of the legal setup. When you apply for the loan for a vacation property, consider it a second home if you are getting a mortgage. However, when you meet with your accountant, you would consider that property an investment property. The IRS looks at that two different ways.

Remember with a second home you cannot rent it more than 14 days a year. Once you do that, it will become an investment property for you.

We will talk more about this in the legal matters chapter, but you can put your property in a dual member LLC. If you're married, your dual member LLC would include you and your spouse. Once it's put into an LLC, you can set up your merchant accounts for your credit cards at the bank with that particular LLC. All the payments that comes to you would go into that LLC. It gives you personal liability coverage that is important in addition to your insurances. Also, it gives you the opportunity to run your vacation property as a business. You'll set it up as that with your accountant.

I strongly encourage you to speak with your attorney and put your vacation property into an LLC. That gives you added protection, and the tax consequences are good because the tax benefits of owning the property flow directly to you. For example, in what is called a *C-corp*, you're actually taxed on the C-corporation, and then any money that comes to you, you're taxed on as well. In an LLC, you're not taxed twice.

Please note that mortgage companies will not loan to an LLC. You will need to place it in an LLC after you have closed on the loan. Remember, lenders do not like this, and most mortgage loan covenants have a *due on sales clause* that could be triggered. This means the mortgage company could make your entire loan due and payable in 30 days. My advice is to consult with your attorney before doing this.

Personal Use

The next key thing is to remain in control of your property for your personal use. One of the reasons that you buy the vacation property to start with, is to use it. Some people will purchase a property and only use it for a week or two out of every year for 10 years. In this case, it makes sense to turn it completely over to a management company as long as you're not trying to maximize your profit. If you want to maximize your profit, then renting it yourself and contracting with the management company for the other services is your best option.

However, I think it's important that you remain in control of your personal use. If you put it completely with a management company, then you need to make sure you have reserved the weeks you want ahead of time. Memories are made at holidays and special times. I believe that vacation properties are an important opportunity and an important vehicle you can use so to maximize your family time and experiences together.

Advertise

It's important that you're willing to spend money to advertise your property. You can invest in advertising no more than $300-$500 a year, and by doing so, the traffic comes to you. Magazines and local newspapers can also be advertisements for your property.

The key to this is making your advertising appealing. For example, www.VRBO. com allows you to post up to 12 photos on your particular listing. Make sure you take quality pictures from a good angle so people can see themselves in the picture experiencing what your listing has to offer. Put in pin markers on your pictures to show clearly see where you're located. You'll also want to show people how close your property is to the beach, show, ski lift, or other feature.

I personally own a European-style home in Colorado, and the balcony looks down on the heart of the village. I have another property that is very private where people could sit out and enjoy beautiful mountains views. In my listing, I showed a photo that displayed how very serene and quiet my property is. People want to know what they're renting before they get there, and that includes the environment and the feel of the property.

Describe all the positive attributes of a property. For example, in an ad for one of my properties, I put "free wireless high-speed internet," "this luxury space is a 1,220-square foot, two-bedroom, two-bath condominium located in the heart of…," "this unit is the best-located, finest two-bedroom in all of this particular village," "it's a one-of-a-kind property, views, views, views, with 15 windows wrapping from east to west, simply the best and quickest access." It's important to include about the access. I put "quick access to everything, steps to the gondola, shopping, restaurants, a general store." I list all those things! "Starbucks, you name it, you can be in the center of the action." Then I talk about how you can sit on the couch and watch the skiers coming down the ski slopes. It's important that you make your property sound appealing whenever you write.

Another key to a great advertisement is to use keywords in the headlines. For example: "Huge luxury condo! Amazing ski views! Incredible location!" Include pictures that show how luxurious and large the condo is. Include views and images of the actual location. There are certain words that literally put people at your place in their minds. You will discover what some of those words are, but it helps tremendously to describe with emotion what the renter will experience in your property.

One of the things that we talk about all the time is the quick access and how convenient something is. You can use terms like "relaxing," "private," or "spacious." One of the things I like to say is "loaded with amenities." Use words that will cause people to buy nights at your property.

Clear Communication

Make sure your contact information is very clear in the online posting. One of the things I really like about using these websites is you are able to communicate primarily through email. In fact, you're able to book and rent through email.

It's important to list the minimum nights you require. For example, we have certain times of the year where there is only a three-night minimum. At the higher demand times, we put five-night minimum. One key is to make sure you price the rental right. For example, weekends like Memorial Day or July 4th are key time periods for a beach property. On those weekends, you can charge more than you would other times. You also can increase your minimum nights during that time.

Perhaps the most important tip is that you must handle your inquiries promptly. If someone emails you about the property, respond to them by email. If they call you about the property, then respond by phone. You need to be able to communicate with a person however they communicated with you. Even if your property isn't available at the time they're requesting it, you still need to answer promptly and professionally.

As we talk about how to maximize your profits and manage vacation properties, it's important that you clearly know what you want to accomplish with your property. One thing my wife and I have agreed to when it comes to our properties is that we're able to have access and use as we want.

Ask yourself what you really want to get out of your property. Are you trying to make a profit? Do you want to hold it for retirement? Is it something you want to use personally? Answer those questions, and you will find yourself enjoying your vacation property much more than someone who has not identified his or her goals.

PART FOUR

CHAPTER 10

HOW TO INSPECT A PROPERTY

Inspecting properties you own or are considering is incredibly important. You want to know exactly what you're getting into and how much you'll have to spend on repairs. I've learned all this from the school of hard knocks.

Interior Inspection

I've had many problems in some of the interiors of our properties including **water damage,** which primarily comes from leaking roofs. Whenever I go into a house, one of the things I look for on the interior is visible water stain marks on the ceilings, the carpets, or the floors. I know that it's coming from either leaking roofs or plumbing problems. One of the greatest problem areas you have in owning properties is bathtubs and showers. In all our properties, we've begun to use sliding doors on the showers instead of shower curtains. Shower curtains can leak over a period of time, which comes through the ceiling and causes lots of problems. At that point, you have sheetrock to replace as well as flooring around the bathtub or the shower.

Of course, if a house was built before 1978, you must look for **lead-based paint**. Usually, it can be remedied by just painting over it with the right kind of paint. If there is scraping that has to be done, then there is a little more mitigation that must go on.

I can tell you, depending on what kind of house you're buying, **windows** can end up being a great cost. One of the things you want to do is to just have the windows repaired, but in some cases, they need to be replaced. You must be able to buy the property at a low enough price to factor in window replacement, which can run anywhere from $250 up to $325. If you have 20 windows in a house, you can see that adds up in a hurry. So, you're looking for operational windows that are already in great shape.

You must also **evaluate the appliances**. Most of the time, if you're buying bargain properties you have to replace them. You really need a good appliance supplier to get you nice appliances at a discounted price.

Some investors overlook **cabinets and counters**. Most of the time, you can actually repair cabinets in the kitchen and the bathroom. But if you're flipping the property, then it's good to replace cabinets and counters.

When we get to major repairs like plumbing, it's important to look for **leaks**. Look underneath the house and in the walls for water stains. Look for linoleum that's peeling up, and look under sinks to see if there are any water stains. Water damage is the number-one problem you deal with as far as the mechanical systems are concerned.

It's also important to inspect for **electrical problems**. In some of the older houses, you'll find aluminum wiring. I prefer not to buy homes with aluminum wiring, but I won't walk away from them just because they have it. Look at the electrical panels both outside and, in some cases, inside. Check your plugs to make sure they're operational. I've spent a lot of money on heating and cooling depending on what part of the country the property was in. You should make sure you're looking at all the systems of the house—heating and cooling, electrical, and plumbing.

Exterior Inspection

First and foremost, inspect the **roof**. How much life is left on it? Look for discolored sections, leaks around vents, and especially sagging roofs. That means either the home is older or the construction wasn't as proper as it should be. Look at the ridgeline and the rafters, and see where the roof may be sagging. Roofs can be very expensive to repair or replace. You want to know how much life is left, because if you know you will need to replace the roof, you must make sure you're buying the house at a value where that's factored in.

Consider the **time frame** for repairs. You don't want any more than about three weeks of time maximum to get a property prepared to be rented or put on the market.

Look at the **chimney**. I once looked at a property that had 17 small chimneys on the roof, and they all needed to be replaced. When I added up all the numbers, no matter who I used to do the work, it just became too expensive. If there are structural problems, chimneys will lean from the house. They can leak as well.

You also need to look at the **siding**. What kind does it have? Does it need to be covered or replaced? Can the house be painted? Does it need to be painted?

Then look at the **foundation**. In different parts of the country, houses are on different foundations. Some houses are actually on a concrete slab, but because of soil problems, the foundation might need to be leveled. You need to factor that into costs as well. In other parts of the country, houses are built on beams, so you want to look for termite problems. Look for bad beams and dry rot.

Septic tanks need to be inspected too. If you're out in rural areas, you want to make sure that they are in proper working order.

These are just some of the areas you need to inspect when evaluating the value of a bargain property. If not inspected correctly, these issues can be huge expenses.

Cosmetic Repairs: Exterior

You're looking for properties that can be "lipsticked," which primarily amounts to cosmetic repairs. This usually entails paint, carpet, maybe a little bit of cabinet work, tile, and other minor fixes. In other words, you're looking for properties that can be spruced up.

You really don't want to spend more than about $3,000-$5,000 on a house. If you're getting into much higher value houses, that number would go up proportionately. On the smaller $100,000 houses, though, you're looking for $3,000-$5,000 to spend. If you're going to flip a house, your goal is $10,000 for every $100,000 invested. That's minimum. You want to make a net profit after your carrying costs and expenses of $10,000.

The work needs to be done in three weeks or less. Ideally, if you're going to flip or sell a house, you need to be able to get it done in a week. I know sometimes that's not realistic, depending on the property, but time is money. It's important when you're looking at these properties that you know what you're doing.

What can you do to spruce up a house? Let's talk about **landscaping** on the exterior first. Of course, get rid of the overgrown bushes, and put in fresh, smaller bushes that make the house look new. Plant new flowers, put in some new bark, mulch, and rock. This will give it a fresh look.

You want the exterior to look fresh. One of the most powerful things you can do to is to **paint** the trim, the front door, the shutters, and the garage door a proper contrasting color that freshens up the house and makes it pop. It gives it curb appeal. If a house does not have shutters, put shutters on it. In most cases, without exception, shutters tremendously add value.

Another thing that adds pizzazz is **new exterior trim lights**. You can do them in brass, white, or black. Put the right kind of lighting in them; I personally like the soft yellow lighting at night that really makes the house glow. All these things can be done on the exterior without a lot of expense while making a tremendous impact on the property itself.

Cosmetic Repairs: Interior

As for the interior, the first step is to **clean everything**. Remove all debris, clean the windows, and get all the grime and the gunk off the property. Obviously, if the carpets are soiled then get out all stains. Get everything out that is not clean—either clean it or remove it.

One of the biggest keys is **paint**. Either use an interior decorator or you come up with a color scheme for your houses. Most of the time you can have one to three schemes and use them in every house. For example, you can go look at the latest model homes and see what colors they're putting together. Keep it simple.

Use the color palette to make a color board and fix up the property accordingly. With a little bit of money for paint and carpet, you can tremendously change the whole look and feel of the interior. Of course, get new floors. Get carpet and tile that fits the color board.

New **fixtures** are important as well. I did this recently with a more high-end property that I was selling. I put new kitchen and bath faucets in and high-end type fixtures. The first thing the lady saw was the high-end kitchen faucet. Make sure that you use your money where you get the best bang for the buck.

Also, you can refurbish or replace the kitchen and the bath **cabinets.** If I'm going to rent out a property, I want to repair, paint, or stain the cabinets unless they're completely torn up. If I'm going to flip or sell a property, I run the numbers for new cabinets, countertops, sinks, and faucets. I compare that to how much I believe I would get out of increased value. If it's not a big difference, I won't do it. Sometimes you can turn a $5,000 investment and get $10,000 more out of the house.

The first thing that makes a property distressed is the condition of the property. You want to learn how to look at properties, determine their value, and inspect them so you know exactly what you're getting into. You also want to have good knowledge about how to fix them up.

CHAPTER 11

LEGAL MATTERS IN REAL ESTATE

Legal matters usually are not the first thing on a new investors mind. However, the experienced investor has learned that making sure he or she is legally and properly covered is a very important part of the real estate business. Begin with an attorney to advise you on how to set up your business and an accountant who understands how to best do your taxes, so you don't get in legal trouble with the IRS. This is how I set up my real estate business for legal protection.

Bill Bronchick, who wrote the foreword for this book, is an attorney and author of six books on real estate. He teaches in our workshops and coaching programs and has developed a brilliant way to legally organize your real estate investments.

Family Limited Partnerships

Investopedia says this: "A Family Limited Partnership (FLP) is a type of arrangement in which family members pool money to run a business project. Each family member buys units or shares of the business and can profit in proportion to the number of shares he or she owns, as outlined in the partnership operating agreement."

Key Takeaways

- An FLP is a business or holding company owned by two or more family members in which each family member can buy shares in the venture for a potential profit.

- There are two types of partners in an FLP: general partners and limited partners.

- FLPs are commonly set up to preserve generational wealth within a family, allowing for tax-free transfers of assets, real estate, and other wealth.

Most FLPs are set up with the partnership consisting of a husband and wife. The FLP easily facilitates the children also being a part of the partnership whenever the time is right. The FLP would then be the single member (own and control) of the LLC.

Limited Liability Company

An LLC is exactly what it says it is; it limits liability you are exposed to. It is difficult for someone who is suing you, let's say a tenant who slips and falls, to actually penetrate the LLC. The person's attorney has to get what is referred to as a *charging order* in order to penetrate what is held within the LLC itself. The limited liability company is a great shield for protecting you personally from liability. All you need is one bad lawsuit, and you have lost everything you have worked years to build.

A limited liability company is also advantageous as a management structure. You can have an unlimited number of members, and you can always change your structure by adding new members and managing members. An LLC can be taxed as a corporation or a partnership. For real estate purposes, being taxed as a partnership has more advantages.

Land Trusts

For maximum protection, each property then should be titled in its own land trusts. The LLC becomes the trustee (owned and controlled by the LLC) of the land trust.

Investopedia states this about a land trust: "A *title-holding trust* [that] allows the property owner to anonymously maintain all rights over the property and direct the actions of the land trust...Not all 50 states have a legal structure in place for a title-holding land trust. However, most states defer to the 'Illinois land trust' laws if they don't have their own, meaning that any individual can form an 'Illinois-style' land trust in any state with proper legal guidance."

I no longer own low-to-moderate income real estate, which as I have stated is a great place to start for the beginning wealth builder. Today, I own more luxury-level properties, including rental properties. I hold individual properties in land trusts, and the Master LLC owns or controls the land trust.

Tax Benefits

Another benefit to setting up an FLP that owns an LLC and the LLC owns each land trust that each property is in, is the tax benefits. This is a big one because tax benefits flow through to you as the members of the LLC. In my case, they actually flow through to my master LLC, and that master LLC flows to me personally through the trust. A C-Corp, on the other hand, is really taxed twice because it has to pay taxes on the earnings it makes as a corporation and any income you received personally from that corporation is taxed as well. That's a huge disadvantage. In an LLC, the income flows through to you as an individual, and you are only taxed one time on that income.

Depreciation flows through to you personally which the government lets you count as a loss. It's really not a loss in your pocket, but you are able to count it as a loss. In a single member LLC, you don't have to file a tax return, but you do have to list it.

An LLC also helps in estate planning. It can provide a vehicle for passing wealth to your younger family members without having to retitle the real estate. Once the real estate is transferred into an LLC, the members' interest is converted to personal property that is represented by shares that are in the LLC. These shares can be transferred and given to your children incrementally up to $10,000 per year, tax-free. The process for transferring the shares is very simple compared to filing a new deed every year, and you can still retain control as the manager of the LLC.

Mortgage Companies and LLCs

Mortgage companies do not like to lend money to entities. When you get loans from mortgage companies, you must get the loan in your name. Again, this is why having a good credit score is so important. We receive loans as individuals, then after we close on properties, we transfer those properties into an LLC.

Mortgage companies are concerned about getting paid. They don't want to loan to an LLC because if you default on your loan payment, they are unsure if they can collect. The fact of the matter is that they have in their contract a *due-on-sale* clause.

The due-on-sale clause is really an acceleration clause. It gives the mortgage company, as the lender, the right to demand immediate payment of whatever is owed when the property is sold. They can still demand full payment if the property is in an LLC.

What people don't realize today is that there is no due-on-sale jail. It is not illegal. To be illegal you must be in violation of criminal law, code, or statute. There is no federal or state law which makes it a crime to violate a due-on-sale clause. If the lender discovers the transfer, they can call the loan due and payable. If you cannot pay, the lender has the option of commencing foreclosure proceedings. So, you have two ways to go: either transfer it back into your personal name or get another loan on the property.

The game for us is how to transfer ownership to the property without getting caught by the lender. You could simply get the owner to sign you a deed and not record it, but this mess is not a good way to go. If the seller gets a judgment or a lien against them, that comes against you.

So, the due-on-sale clause is something that is a gray area for investors. You may wonder why I bring it up here. It's because I'm a big believer in being protected. If you're going to pay the mortgage company what it's owed, the mortgage payment, you take the risk based on the due-on-sale clause. Some of you have to decide if that is right for you in how you're conducting your real estate business.

Many real estate investors do this because it is not against the law. It does provide you with limited liability protection, but you need to be prepared to either transfer the property back into the mortgage company or pay the loan by getting a brand-new loan on the property. In either case, if you're willing to take the risk, having an LLC protects you immensely from lawsuits and other things that can happen from the outside.

If you do not want to do this with a mortgage company, banks will loan money to an LLC as long as you make the payment. Some banks do not even require that you personally sign for the loan. If the limited liability company does not pay, the bank comes after you because they require the personal guarantee. It's as if you were cosigning a loan.

Property Insurance

Make sure you are getting title insurance. Title insurance will cost you up to 1% of the loan amount, but it's important. I'm very aggressive about this and the title companies I work with know that.

I had a situation happen out on the East Coast where we purchased a property and paid for the title insurance; everything was in order. There was a bill (a lien) against the property that the title insurance company did not pick up on for $900. The lien was placed by the city on the property. We simply picked up the phone, called the title company that issued the insurance, and they had to pay the $900 to satisfy the lien.

I knew of a person who bought a commercial piece of property and he did not have title insurance. He discovered there were 17 different liens against the property that totaled much more than the property was worth. Obviously, he got himself into trouble. Title insurance is critically important for every property you purchase.

Hazard insurance that includes lost-rents coverage is also incredibly important. I had a property that had a kitchen fire, and the hazard insurance more than covered the claims. We were able to fix it up and sell it. The insurance company will pay two to three months of lost-rents coverage, which means you will not lose any income on the property while it's being repaired. That's a key thing to know.

Even if you have LLC protection, I advise you to get a million-dollar umbrella liability policy that covers you. You really can't be over-insured when you're in this business, so by receiving an umbrella liability protection and policy, you get an additional protective layer.

You also need to have workmen's compensation insurance for the contractors working on your properties. If their workers get hurt on your property, they can come after you. You can fight that because you have the limited liability company protection, but it's a whole lot safer to make sure they show you they actually have workmen's compensation before you let them work on your property.

Flood insurance is also important. You need to know before you ever place an offer on a property if you are in a floodplain where the government automatically requires you to purchase flood insurance. What investors don't realize is that flood insurance is expensive, and it can take you out of the positive cash flow. You can factor the flood insurance into the amount you charge for rent in order to maintain a positive cash flow, but you have to be aware.

Management Company

Legal matters in investing are incredibly important. This is why I am very comfortable having a management company. I know a lot of real estate investors do not use management companies because the majority of real estate investors in America own five or fewer properties. If you have a goal or a dream to get much larger that and developing a cash flow of $100,000 a year tax-free, you definitely want to use a management company.

You probably should manage your first property or two, but do not let that distract you from building your real estate portfolio if you have bigger dreams. It's critical that you hire a management company so you're able to spend your time and energy acquiring properties. Most of the time, you have to pay 8-10% in management fees.

One of the reasons I like to use management companies is because they take care of the late-night calls to fix the plumbing. They also handle all evictions for tenants who don't pay their rent, which is another legal matter. The reason I bring the management company up in the legal matters portion is that they know the judges, the individual courts, and the procedures in that particular state. This means they know how to file an eviction notice. That's so important for two reasons. First of all, you don't want to consume your time and energy doing that. Second of all, you want to make sure you handle the eviction notice correctly.

Legal Risks

Let me bring up some of the potential risks of owning and overseeing your properties. The first one, of course, is the bad tenant. When screening a tenant, do background and credit checks as well as visiting their current residence to see how they take care of their property. I also encourage you to call their past two landlords and check any references they've listed on the rental application. You need to have them fill out a detailed rental application, which you can find in the appendix of this manual.

Most landlords are really good-hearted people who don't address delinquent rents immediately, but the one area you cannot compromise on at all is paying rent. People go through difficult times, and you can definitely help them. But find other ways to do that rather than sacrificing their rent payment. If you let them default on their rent, you will create a codependent behavior with your tenant where they expect you to cover their rent for them. You have to be very careful with that.

Make sure that you enforce all policies immediately. If you don't allow pets and tenants don't obey that, immediately ask them to remove the pet. Sometimes it's heartbreaking, but the tenants knew you did not accept pets before they ever moved in.

Always make sure that you require a security deposit and the first and last month's rent. That keeps tenants from moving out unnecessarily, and if they've done harm to the property you have a security deposit for that.

You also need to complete a statement of condition and have the tenant sign it. When a tenant moves in, you actually put this as an addendum to the lease. Attach the form, go through the property, and talk about everything. Make it clear that there are no repairs that are currently needed, and everything is good working order. Make sure to also put the cost of what repairs would be on the sheet.

For example, if there is a stopped-up toilet, tell them how much it will cost. Many tenants will expect you to fix it, so they don't have to pay it. We don't allow that. If they want, they can add the repair costs to next month's rent.

If they do not pay, you can begin the eviction process. You're in good shape because you've got a security deposit and first and last month's rent. When you complete a statement of condition, have the tenant sign it and then have a list of repairs that outline how much everything costs.

Another potential risk in holding real estate is refinancing a property, which I am a big advocate for. Why is that a potential risk? A lot of investors miss what is called a *pre-payment penalty*. If you refinance a property within 12-36 months (some pre-payment penalties go as long as 60 months), they charge you a very high rate, sometimes 2-3% of the loan amount. You will have to pay off if you want to sell the property or refinance it.

In most cases, it is much wiser for a real estate investor to pay a higher interest rate in order to avoid the pre-payment penalty.

Most of the time, newer real estate investors become obsessed with the interest rates. No one wants to pay a higher interest rate than they should. However, there are times when it makes just good business sense. You lose your flexibility to refinance your properties if you have a high pre-payment penalty. You have to weigh your options, but do not be concerned or afraid to pay the higher interest rate as long as it's not way out there. Don't step over dimes to pick up pennies!

I think it's important that your managers check your properties once a month and provide you with an inspection report. If you're an out-of-state owner, I believe you should go see your properties every 90 days. Aggressively inspect the inside, and if you have a tenant who is not taking care of your properties, talk to your manager about getting that tenant out.

Real estate is less liquid than most investments, meaning you're not going to blow your money because you have some extra cash. It usually takes a year of seasoning to be able to refinance properties and get cash out of them. It is much easier to do a cash-out refinance than it has ever been because of the computerized lending. However, it is less liquid. That definitely can be an advantage as much as it is a risk.

There are also long-term costs of owning property to consider. There is 100% return if you buy the properties as we show you how to buy them, but there is still cost in owning property. A lot of people don't realize it takes 21 years to pay half of the principal balance of a 30-year loan. I prefer to receive the cash flow.

Though there are certain risks to owning real estate, the reward far outweighs it. In this chapter, I showed you all the best ways I know to protect myself and my investments. Again, legal matters can get tricky, but don't let that discourage you. Real estate is the best investment I have ever made.

PART FIVE

CHAPTER 12

| FIXING AND FLIPPING

The best way to build wealth with real estate is buying and holding real estate. In other words, you buy it, repair it, hold it for a while (seven to 10 years), and then, in most cases, you can increase your real estate holdings by utilizing a 1031 Exchange and buy a larger property without incurring any capital gains taxes. This can be done an unlimited number of times as you continue to purchase larger properties.

Additionally, if you're an active investor, you will always be looking for more property. So, there will be times when you come across a property that will serve you better from a financial perspective to fix and flip it. That would mean you kill the tree that is producing fruit, but you receive cash immediately from the sale instead of waiting for it to produce rental income.

Here's the way it works. You buy and hold your first house, and then you buy another house also to rent it. Remember, now you're buying and holding. You may even buy and hold as many as three houses because you have enough money for the down payment and the repairs, but you start running low on cash. Then on the fourth house, you actually buy that house and sell it in order to generate more cash.

When I do this, the number-one question I ask myself is, "Do I need the cash?" In other words, do I need the amount of cash this house will produce if I sell it? The second question besides needing the cash is, "Would this property serve me better short term as a flipper? Could I make a least $20,000 for every $100,000 I invested?"

There are houses all along the way as I was building my portfolio that I would buy for the purpose of flipping—either to get more cash or the house easily met the flipping formula. Also, I knew I could sell it quickly because it would be desirable for someone to purchase.

As a real estate investor, you need at least two or three streams of income or more. Obviously, the primary income stream in real estate (what I did) is to buy and hold: buy property, get the cash flow to be positive from rent (which I have been teaching you in this book), and then take that excess cash flow and pocket it or buy more houses.

But then, there comes a time you will need another income stream, and one way to obtain it is to fix and flip a house. There are some people I know who have been in our workshops or courses and all they do as a business is fix and flip.

Now remember, if you fix and flip, you pay more in taxes than when you buy and hold. So, everything that I taught you on the buy and hold and how rent is classified as passive income, changes when you fix and flip. So always remember this: if you buy a property and sell that property in less than 12 months, you must pay earned income tax on it. It's not passive. It's not capital gains. It's earned income. If you buy a property and you flip it, then you will be in a higher tax bracket on the earnings than on rental income.

The best strategy is to combine buy and hold and fix and flip. This combining strategy enables you to build wealth for the long term (buy and hold), create income streams (through both), raise cash as you need it (flipping), and protect your income from unnecessary taxes (buy and hold).

Fix and Flip Questions to Ask

1. Have you considered your options for financing?

I have mentioned financing throughout this chapter. Remember, when flipping you are not holding the property for long so you would not use mortgage financing. Some of the options you might consider are listed below.

a. **HELOC**—Many people who buy and flip will use the equity in their home. HELOC means "home equity line of credit," and it functions as a true line of credit. You only borrow what you need to purchase and rehab, and when you sell, you pay it back and use the money for the next buy and flip. The good news is that you do not have to pay it back, but you can use it immediately for another flip. It is flexible and cheap compared to other sources of financing. The other big advantage is that you only pay interest when you actually use the money.

b. **SECOND MORTGAGE**—Another good alternative is a second mortgage on your home. However, this loan starts generating interest the minute it closes, and the monthly payment costs stay the same until it is paid off. I actually used this method of financing to get me started in real estate investing. The other negative is that the interest rates on these loans are higher than a HELOC or a first mortgage.

c. **BORROWING AGAINST YOUR IRA**—For many reading this book, this can be a good choice especially if it is used with other alternatives. Of course, you can use the cash that you borrow to pay cash for the property and rehab of your real estate investment. Or you could just borrow the down payment from your IRA and use a bank for the remainder needed to purchase and rehab the property.

d. **INVESTING WITH YOUR IRA**—The highest and best way to do this is to set up a self-directed IRA that invests into a company you own (an LLC) and the company buys the real estate. We instruct you how to do this in our Real Estate Mastery Course on our website WBUNIVERSITY.online. Also, there is an option to invest directly from your IRA without setting up the company, but the guideline requirements for most investors are way too arduous.

e. **LOCAL BANK**—For purposes of instruction to the reader our thoughts are to avoid at all costs the larger brand-name banks and focus on the small family banks that do real estate lending. These are difficult to Google, so you have to visit them one by one to see how real estate friendly they are. In addition, one of the most important things I will tell you in this entire book is that most banks do not service your real estate loan if it is a mortgage. They sell the paper to one of the quasi-government agencies like Fannie Mae or Freddie Mac. However, if you go in telling them that you want to buy and flip, they may loan you the money and service your loan. These kind of "portfolio" loans are much more flexible than standard mortgages. The banker will want to know in the beginning how much cash and income you have along with your credit score and real estate investing experience. I built much of my portfolio with this type of lending, and after I became more established, I would do 100% loans for the purchase and rehab of property.

f. **PRIVATE PARTY LENDER**—Some people have money they would like to lend on real estate. Several years ago, I met with one investor who had a radio program he did on the weekends advertising particular properties he was targeting to purchase. He was offering a good interest rate (8% when interest rates were 6% on a regular 30-year mortgage) on a first mortgage with an 80% loan-to-value against the as-repaired appraisal of the house. Let's say the house needed some work and the sellers were asking $100,000 due to financial distress. In this example, they owe $60,000 on the house. He offers them $80,000 cash (he already has a private lender in place), and he can close in 10 days. They accept his offer to get out from the load of the house payment. He purchases the house for $80,000 and invests $15,000 into it for rehab. The as-repaired appraisal in this example is now $120,000. An 80% first mortgage on the new as-repaired appraisal is $96,000. The private party lender lends the investor $96,000 on a first mortgage with which he spends $80,000 to purchase it, and $15,000 to rehab it. The property purchaser received a 100% loan to do the deal. There was *no money out of pocket and "nothing down."* In most cases, the investors would sell the house and pay the lender back. Most private lenders will put a limit that requires the loan be at least for several years so they can make more interest. In that case, the investor rents the property for three years before he sells it.

g. **HARD MONEY LENDERS**—Hard money lenders are lenders that charge higher interest rates (12%-16% annually) and usually two points when the loan is made. If we use the example above, the investor could still purchase and rehab the property and sell it in the 90 days using a hard money lender with none of his own money. The hard money lender would be willing to lend the $95,000 for purchase and repair. The investor would need to pay him back at the time the house sold, $1900 (2 points) plus $3800 interest. The investor made approximately $20,000 in this illustration when the house sold and had none of his own money in the deal. Note: some hard money lenders require the points upfront by tasking it out of the amount they loan. Also, they require the investor to have some of his money in the deal.

h. **FRIENDS AND FAMILY**—You may have family or friends who want to invest with you, and it gives them an opportunity to make a decent return on their money. The loan principles that you use in other types should be your guide here. The difference with family and friends would be that it may be much easier to not have to use any of your own money. Just remember to always them pay back on the terms you agreed upon.

2. Can I make $20,000 profit for every $100,000 invested?

If you decide to include fixing and flipping in your real estate strategy, then remember the guideline mentioned above to aim for a minimum of 20% profit. This means for every $100,000 invested; you make a profit of $20,000. Some markets may be more difficult to reach this amount of profit and some may actually be better. Remember, if you consider combining this strategy with buying and holding, for every three houses you locate, one may need to be a flipper, depending on your cash needs.

3. Do you know where the real estate market is in regard to the real estate cycle?

Earlier, we looked at how important it is to know where you are in the real estate cycle if you're considering flipping as a strategy. The best times to flip are when supply is beginning to decrease, and demand is beginning to increase. It is best to look back on the past five years of supply. The way I like to study supply and demand is to investigate how many houses were for sale on June 1st of the past five years. Then study what prices did during that time. The best time to fix and flip is when demand is escalating and prices are increasing. Of course, it is difficult to always catch the cycles perfectly. That's why your knowledge and understanding of flipping and building efficient and cost-effective teams are so important. You can still make money in tighter markets with increased personal real estate know-how and highly torqued rehabbed teams.

4. How well do you know the area?

I learned how important this is when I began to look at new areas to purchase more real estate. As I began to look at an area in the southern states of the U.S., I looked for experienced real estate agents who knew the area but also owned investment property themselves.

I did not know what some of the problems or benefits of the area were so I started calling real estate agents. I asked them, "If you had houses in this area that you would avoid, what would be wrong with them?" Also, "What neighborhoods would you avoid and why?"

The first thing I learned was a lot of houses in that area had what's called *exterior insulation finishing system (EIFS)* stucco. EIFS is a form of stucco made out of Styrofoam, and in areas with a lot of moisture, those properties need to be avoided. Then I found out because there were a lot of trees in the area—and these were really nice houses—the builders would actually bury some of the logs and the trees underneath the foundations. They did not compact the dirt and trees like they should have. The logs would rot, and then the pipes they put in the ground for plumbing (no longer cast iron but plastic) would buckle or sag. This caused major plumbing problems. So today, no matter what part of the country I may be in, I always get a plumbing scope even if I'm buying a property in *as-is* condition.

That was one of the first times I learned to actually do what's called *plumbing scope.* I learned to look and see if there are any dips in the lines. Usually, if the house has been there for a period of time and doesn't have any dips, that's a good sign. I encourage you when you go in to flip to make sure you understand the area and what kind of problems may be common to that particular area.

5. Does the home conform to mortgage guidelines for lending?

Will the investment property conform to FHA lending guidelines after repairs? Since the Great Recession (2008-2011), the FHA requires certain kinds of repairs to be done on a house that they previously did not require. So, for example, if you're looking to flip and you buy a house aimed at first-time homeowners, the FHA would probably be a common loan the person would need. It's not what you need, but what the buyer needs to buy your house. So make sure that you do fix it up because now we're talking about a flip, not a buy and hold. With a flip, you need to be able to sell it fast.

6. Will you make money when you buy?

Always remember as we've said before, you make money in real estate when you buy, not when you sell. The idea is that when you buy (if you're going to flip), you need a 20% profit potential as I mentioned above. In other words, can you make $20,000 per $100,000? Never buy where the margins are too tight if you're going to flip.

7. Is it a normal neighborhood?

I intentionally listed this question here to tell you to avoid commercial or industrial areas, crime areas, and even areas that have apartments. We're talking about flipping here—not about buying and holding. When flipping is the goal, you want to be in that bread-and-butter, Mister Rogers' neighborhood in order to flip quickly and successfully. In other words, it needs to be a solid neighborhood with good families. Don't buy, for example, in a neighborhood where businesses are kind of filtering in. I've seen those kinds of neighborhoods turn over and become commercial. Sometimes they're worth more, but we're talking about a goal of flipping. We're not talking about buying and holding. So make sure you are selling a property in an area that your target buyer desires.

Also, when I evaluate a neighborhood, I always visit the area at night. In fact, let me tell you something. Before you buy a house, especially one you're going to flip, learn to sit in the house. Sit down in the house at night, and do the same thing during the day. Learn to sit down, look around, and always ask realtors wherever the house is, "Can I come in at night?" If I'm really serious about purchasing a property and I'm going to spend some real money, I especially want to see the house at night. I want to sit in the house, and see what the light looks like coming in from the outside. I want to hear the sounds and see if there is any noise pollution. I want to determine if I hear any weird noises, experience anything strange, or see weird lights coming in from somewhere I didn't know about. That may sound strange to you, and I understand. But remember, the goal here is that you want to buy properties that you can sell quickly, so you don't want any surprises. Any buyer will want to feel safe at night.

8. Can the renovations be done in 60 days or less?

The whole idea between fixing and flipping is you must be in and out quickly. The best flips are when you're in and out in 30 days and the house is listed. One step better would be that you buy the house, 10 days later you get a contract on the house because you've already started renovating it, somebody looks at it and likes the renovations you're doing, and you actually close on that house 45 days after you bought it. That should be a large profit flip!

The goal is to get all your rehab done and get it on the market because *time is money*. So the longer that you're in a property if you're borrowing money to buy it, then the more interest you're paying while you're holding that property.

9. Is the property being sold in as-is condition?

That's okay as long as you know what you're doing and you have good inspector. It's also important that you personally understand what it will take to rehab it and you know that you're taking a risk when you buy as-is. You can't come back on the seller for something you find wrong with the house later. Also, it's really important if you're buying a property as-is to still get a thorough inspection done so you really understand what needs to be done to the property. Your rehab contractors need to thoroughly inspect the property before you buy so you understand all of your costs.

10. Can I inspect the home prior to closing?

The only reason this question is included here is because I see people at auctions buying foreclosures they've never seen, but they expect to flip them quickly and profitably. One of the things you must be really careful about is if you're going to flip, you need to be able to inspect the house carefully and also have an inspection done before you buy it.

11. Is the average sales time for the neighborhood less than 90 days?

This is a big one. You're looking for neighborhoods that are desirable. If you examine the comparison sales through websites like Zillow.com or Realtor.com, you can see how long houses in a particular neighborhood stayed on the market. You can also see how long the property you are considering has been on the market and whether it has been relisted for sale and the tally for the number of days on the market has been started over. But, generally speaking, take into consideration how many days it takes for properties to sell in a particular neighborhood. Don't buy to flip in neighborhoods that on the average take longer than 90 days to sell.

12. Have you confirmed the as-repaired appraisal amount?

One of the things that's critical is whether or not you've found lenders that will do as-repaired appraisals and lend accordingly. If you use a bank or even a hard money lender loan as opposed to a purchase mortgage, will they allow you to set repair money aside in escrow so you're able to draw on that money as you need it for repairs? The same question is necessary to ask of a regular mortgage lender. You may have to take a few extra steps. So, what you're really looking for is what the number would be on the as-repaired appraisal. That tells you realistically what you think you can sell the house for. Sometimes that appraisal comes in a little less than what you can actually sell it for. But make sure you can get your repair money in the mortgage loan, so you don't have to come up with that cash.

13. Do you have a good repair team in place?

I can't emphasize this enough. I always talk about rehab contractors when we talk about the importance of a team. In fact, it's wise to have more than one rehab team. You may find another great buy that you need to move on quickly, and you need another team to rehab it. A word of caution here. Don't buy more properties than you have good teams to handle. Some investors end up sitting on a house sometimes for six months before they can actually get a contractor in it. That's a waste of time and money. More than likely, you won't make any money on that house. Again, I encourage you to have a good repair team or two in place.

14. Have you found a good lender for your buyers?

This is one I learned the most about when I owned a home-building company. I'll have people who own some type of commercial property who call me and say, "Hey, I've got this building somewhere in America I want you to look at, and I'm having a hard time selling it." I'll say, "Have you talked to any professional commercial real estate lenders? Because they can help you with that." Many times, people who purchase commercial real estate don't know how to go about getting a loan for the property they are considering. If you are the seller, it is advantageous to create your own lending relationships so you can help a buyer get approved for financing.

The same thing is true on a single-family house. I'm using the commercial property intentionally as an example because it can be more complicated than single-family property. I remember going to look at one of our coaching client's properties. One of the things I taught him was that if he was flipping manufactured housing (which normally would be not approved for purchase mortgage financing), he had to find banks in that area that would make loans on that kind of property. He listened to me and he would bring those banks to those buyers. If you're going to be a flipper, you need to learn how to get a buyer approved for financing, and you need to know the best mortgage brokers or bankers to send people to.

15. Have you scheduled open houses that you attend?

If you're going to flip, you will learn at open houses what appeals to people—like fresh cookies baking in the oven. Remember, you're flipping now, not holding, and the smells and sounds matter. So, go to open houses and listen to what the other buyers are asking for as you're in the open house just walking around. You can learn a lot about what you need to have in your properties.

16. Are you prepared to stage the property?

Not staging the home is a critical mistake that beginning flippers make. They do not understand the importance of staging the home for potential buyers. One of our coaches in the Wealthbuilders.org real estate coaching program teaches that buyers decide if they will make an offer in the first seven seconds of entering a home. As stated earlier, the look, feel, smell, and sounds of a home for sale are critical. If a buyer cannot see the themselves living in the home, then they will not make an offer. Paint colors should be neutral so not to put off the buyer, and the rooms should be staged so a potential buyer can quickly see their purpose and the amount of space they offer. Find a good professional stager and use their services.

17. What do you repair or improve?

The main goal is to find properties that just need cosmetic improvement. There are enough TV shows on flipping real estate to show what kind cosmetic improvements are needed. You can discover what the "in" neutral colors are pretty quickly. They usually are some kind of beige or gray or a combination of both. Go look at some upscale model homes in a city close to you. They will usually have the right color combinations. In most homes you're going to flip, learn to bring in more light. It typically makes the home more desirable. I don't mean bring in the western sun shining at 200 degrees. I'm talking about bringing in just the light and ambiance in the house. Sometimes you can do it with canisters, but what I'm talking about is outside natural light. Since there is no room for a comprehensive list here just remember anything that has color could be important. There are ways with staging to tone down the bright pink tile in bathroom tile or weird turquoise floor tile in the house. Believe me, it is important! Also focus on the kitchen and the master bathroom. The colors, layout, and conveniences of those spaces will be important. Again, check out the model homes in your area. Also, don't forget about the curb appeal. Landscaping is critical to helping a home sell quickly. Just removing overgrown bushes with fresh shrubs and newly planted flowers makes a big difference. Painting the front door a darker shade than the trim can make the house stand out, and don't forget the shutters.

When it comes to fixing and flipping, one thing you must do upon entering a prospective property is pay attention to any obvious problems and determine how you would fix them. Sometimes the layout is the problem or a repair that's needed to fix something. Especially look over the kitchen and the master bath because that's where you start on flips, and that's where you've got to spend the money. Sometimes you can change a kitchen by simply painting the cabinets. That's not always the case, so if it's not, you need to have a good cabinet company come in to help you. But make sure the kitchen and master bath are right

There are shortcuts. In other words, you can really improve a property, especially with colors. In fact, if you listen to home-staging expert Karen Conrad, she'll tell you how painting with the right colors can best stage your house. (Karen's staging courses are available through Wealthbuilders University, our real estate courses, and youtube.com. For example, if a house has weird turquoise tile, painting with the right colors and staging the place right can downplay a lot of problems. Most of the time when you're flipping, you do need to stage, which I'll reference again.

But remember, among the first things you'll want to do when flipping is to look over how to improve the kitchen and master bath and how to update the colors. As a matter of fact, right now I think the color Bread Crust that we've been talking about among the team is still one of the popular colors. It's kind of a what we call a "grayish-taupe" or a "greige" type color. Another tip is to go look at tiles and fixtures in new construction and see what they're using. That will give you a good idea of the kinds of things that need to be fixed.

A lot of people ask, "What should I fix on the interior?" Sometimes there are design space solutions that can add a lot to a property—everything from closets to more. I had a friend who made a change I thought was brilliant. He bought a beautiful home on a lake, but the home offered no view of the lake. This is a true story. I mean it had one little window in the kitchen. I don't get it. So my friend created a monster window that just looked out on the beautiful lake and featured it. He flipped that house in 30 days for one window. He just changed the whole house by putting in a window. After his changes, one walk in the door and you looked right out over the lake. Why the people before didn't have a window there I'll never know. He bought the house for a good price, flipped it, and made a great profit and some really good money.

So, take a good look at design space solutions and what I call conversions of existing spaces. This would apply to flips as well. As long as it doesn't hurt the use of the space, you also can sometimes add a bedroom or bathroom. Just make sure to take into account the design space solutions we've talked about.

Just as much as the one guy added a window and exposed a great lake view, it just as important to get rid of an undesirable view. Sometimes just a matter of planning some mature landscaping can help or protect the view. Realize there are different ways you can fix things. This is my favorite example, though I kind of hate to tell this story. I knew a person who bought a house for a flip. He was going to live in it for about three months and then flip it. How he missed this I'll never know, but he moved into the house and about the third night he sat straight up in the bed hearing a loud train whistle. Across the street was a track, and the train traveled right passed his house. This was a beautiful luxury home. The guy put in soundproof windows, soundproof drapes. He put in everything you could imagine, and it still didn't reduce the noise.

Guess what? He never flipped the house. Why he didn't do his due diligence on the house beforehand, I'll never understand.

Fixing and flipping is important especially if you want to continue to build your portfolio. One of the ways a lot of people begin this process is by pulling out the equity that is in their primary house. There are three primary ways you can do this:

- Firstly, you can refinance your first mortgage if you have enough equity available. For example, let's say you still owe $100,000 on your home, but it is now worth $200,000. You can refinance with a first mortgage that is 80% of the value of the home. Eighty percent of $200,000 is $160,000. At the time of the refinance, $100,000 goes to pay off the original $100,000 mortgage, and $60,000 goes in your pocket to use to purchase and rehab a property.

- Secondly, a second mortgage would use the same numbers. Let's say the house is worth $200,000. Instead of refinancing the entire mortgage, a second mortgage is issued for $60,000. The net effect is the same as above except the second mortgage would have a little higher interest rate and payment.

- Thirdly, in most states you can use a HELOC (home equity line of credit). The numbers are the same as above, but instead of utilizing a first or second mortgage you would use a HELOC. HELOCs are great because you only pay interest on the amount you borrow up to the $60,000 limit, and the interest rates on HELOCs are always lower than second mortgages. Many times they can be lower than first mortgages.

- As an example, let's say John Doe pulls out $60,000 in equity from his primary house and uses $20,000 for a down payment to buy his first buy-and-hold property. Then he takes $20,000 to use for a down payment on another house. Each is 20% down on a $100,000 house. That leaves him $20,000. He spends $5,000 per house on repairs, which only leaves a total of $10,000 from the original $100,000. When he gets to the third house, he needs to be able to fix it and flip it in order to raise more cash. As an example, let's say he can make $30,000 profit when he sells it. The $30k profit and the remaining $10k added together gives him $40k, which can be used as a down payment for two more houses. One house can be a buy-and-hold, and one house can be a fix and flip. This is how you go about maintaining enough liquidity to continue to purchase properties.

GLOSSARY

1031 Exchange: A section of the U.S. Internal Revenue Service Code that allows investors to defer capital gains taxes on any exchange of like-kind properties for business or investment purposes. Taxes on capital gains are not charged on the sale of a property if the money is being used to purchase another property. The payment of tax is deferred until property is sold with no reinvestment.

Adjustable Rate Mortgages: A variable-rate mortgage or tracker mortgage is a mortgage loan with the interest rate on the note periodically adjusted based on an index which reflects the cost to the lender of borrowing on the credit markets.

Amortization Schedule: An amortization schedule is a complete table of periodic loan payments, showing the amount of principal and the amount of interest that comprise each payment until the loan is paid off at the end of its term.

Appraisal: A written report that estimates the current fair market value of the property that you are buying or selling.

Appreciation: An increase in the value of an asset over time. The increase can occur for a number of reasons, including increased demand or weakening supply, or as a result of changes in inflation or interest rates. This is the opposite of depreciation, which is a decrease over time.

As-Is Condition: As-is denotes that the seller is selling, and the buyer is buying an item in whatever condition it presently exists, and that the buyer is accepting the item "with all faults," whether or not immediately apparent.

As-Repaired Appraisal: An as-repaired appraisal is an estimate of the fair market value of the home after it has been repaired.

Asset: an item of ownership having exchange value.

Capital Gains: An increase in the value of a capital asset that gives it a higher worth than the purchase price. The gain is not realized until the asset is sold.

C-Corp: Refers to any corporation that is taxed separately from its owners.

Collateral: A property or other asset that a borrower offers as a way for a lender to secure the loan.

Contract for Deed: A legal document that grants the bearer a right or privilege, provided that he or she meets a number of conditions.

Contingency Clauses: A contract provision that requires a specific event or action to take place in order for the contract to be considered valid.

Debt to Income Ratio: A personal finance measure that compares an individual's debt payment to his or her overall income.

Depreciation: Depreciation is an accounting method of allocating the cost of a tangible asset over its useful life.

Due on Sale Clause: A provision in a mortgage contract that requires the mortgage to be repaid in full upon a sale or conveyance of partial or full interest in the property that secures the mortgage.

Equity Buy Down: A mortgage-financing technique with which the buyer attempts to obtain a lower interest rate for at least the first few years of the mortgage, but possibly its entire life.

Family Limited Partnership: A Family Limited Partnership (FLP) is a type of arrangement in which family members pool money to run a business project. Each family member buys units or shares of the business and can profit in proportion to the number of shares he or she owns, as outlined in the partnership operating agreement.

FHA Loans: Federal Housing Authority. These are loans designed for low-to-moderate income borrowers who are unable to make a large down payment.

Fixed Rate Mortgages: A fixed-rate mortgage is a mortgage that has a fixed interest rate for the entire term of the loan.

Flipping: Flipping is when a real estate investor purchases a house and, in most instances, repairs it and then sells it quickly for a profit.

Foreclosure: A situation in which a homeowner is unable to make full principal and interest payments on his/her mortgage, which allows the lender to seize the property, evict the homeowner and sell the home, as stipulated in the mortgage contract.

HAP Contract: Housing Assistance Payments. A contract entered into by the landlord and the local housing authority which is funded by HUD setting forth the rights and duties of the parties with respect to the project and the payments under the HAP contract. This contract provides rent assistance to approved renters, in many cases paying 100% of the rent directly to the landlord.

HELOC: A HELOC, or **home equity line of credit**, is a **line of credit** similar to a credit card. With this loan, you can borrow up to a specific amount of your home **equity** and repay the funds slowly over time. HELOCs have a draw period, or a period of time in which you can access the money, that typically lasts around 10 years.

HUD: The Department of Housing and Urban Development (HUD) is a U.S. government agency created in 1965 to support community development and home ownership.

Interest: Interest is the charge for the privilege of borrowing money, typically expressed as annual percentage rate.

IRA: Individual Retirement Account. IRAs are tax-advantaged investing tools for individuals to earmark their retirement savings.

Keogh Plan: A tax-deferred pension plan available to self-employed individuals or unincorporated businesses for retirement purposes. A Keogh plan can be set up as either a defined-benefit or defined-contribution plan, although most plans are set as defined contribution.

Land Contract: An agreement between a buyer and seller of property in which the buyer makes payments toward full ownership (as with a mortgage), but in a land contract, the title or deed is held by the owner until the full payment is made.

Land Trust: A title-holding trust [that] allows the property owner to anonymously maintain all rights over the property and direct the actions of the land trust...Not all 50 states have a legal structure in place for a title-holding land trust. However, most states defer to the "Illinois land trust" laws if they don't have their own, meaning that any individual can form an "Illinois-style" land trust in any state with proper legal guidance.

Lease Option: An agreement that gives a renter the choice to purchase a property during or at the end of the rental period. As long as the lease option period is in effect, the landlord/seller may not offer the property for sale to anyone else.

Lien: A lender's claim to a borrower's collateral.

Lines of Credit: An arrangement between a financial institution, usually a bank, and a customer that establishes a maximum loan balance that the lender permits the borrower to access or maintain.

Liquid Asset: An asset that can be converted into cash quickly, with minimal impact to the price received in the open market.

LLC: Limited Liability Company. A corporate structure whereby the members of the company cannot be held personally liable for the company's debts or liabilities. It can be taxed as a corporation or a partnership.

Series LLC: A series LLC is a unique form of limited liability company in which the articles of formation specifically allow for unlimited segregation of membership interests, assets, and operations into independent series. Each series operates like a separate entity with a unique name, bank account, and separate books and records.

Loan-to-value: A lending risk assessment ratio that financial institutions and other lenders examine before approving a mortgage.

Mortgage Banker: A company, individual or institution that originates mortgages. Mortgage bankers use their own funds, or funds borrowed from a warehouse lender, to fund mortgages.

Mortgage Broker: A mortgage broker gathers paperwork from a borrower and passes that paperwork along to a mortgage lender for underwriting and approval. The mortgage funds are lent in the name of the mortgage lender, and the mortgage broker collects an origination fee from the lender as compensation for services.

Net Worth: The amount by which your assets exceed liabilities.

No Document Loan: A loan that gives borrowers the ability to state a limited amount of information on their mortgage application.

Portfolio Lender: A company that not only originates mortgage loans, but also holds a portfolio of their loans instead of selling them off in the secondary market.

Pre-approval Letter: With pre-approval, you will receive a conditional commitment in writing for an exact loan amount, allowing you to look for a home at or below that price level.

Pre-qualification Letter: You supply a bank or lender with your overall financial picture, including your debt, income and assets. After evaluating this information, a lender can give you an idea of the mortgage amount for which you qualify.

Principal Interest: The amount of interest one pays on a loan is determined by the principal sum.

Public Housing Authority: Administered by federal, state, and local agencies to provide subsidized assistance for low-income households.

Purchase Mortgage: A mortgage issued to the borrower by the seller of a home as part of the purchase transaction.

Real Estate Professional Designation: To be a real estate professional, a taxpayer must provide more than one-half of his or her total personal services in real property trades or businesses in which he or she materially participates and performs more than 750 hours of services during the tax year in real property trades or businesses.

Refinance Mortgage: Getting a new mortgage to replace the original which allows a borrower to obtain a better interest term and rate.

Section 8 Housing: Section 8 of the Housing Act of 1937 authorizes the payment of rental housing assistance to private landlords on behalf of low-income households in the United States.

Self-Directed IRA: A self-directed individual retirement account (SDIRA) is a type of individual retirement account that can hold a variety of alternative investments normally prohibited from regular IRAs. Although the account is administered by a custodian or trustee, it's directly managed by the account holder—the reason it's called *self-directed.*

SEP (simplified employee pension plan): A simplified employee pension (SEP or SEP IRA) is a retirement plan that an employer or self-employed individual can establish. The employer is allowed a tax deduction for contributions made to the SEP plan and makes contributions to each eligible employee's SEP IRA on a discretionary basis.

Settlement Statement: A settlement statement is a document that summarizes the terms and conditions of a loan agreement. A loan settlement statement provides full disclosure of a loan's terms, but most importantly it details all of the fees and charges that a borrower must pay extraneously from a loan's interest.

Short Sale: A short sale in real estate is when a financially distressed homeowner sells his or her property for less than the amount due on the mortgage. The buyer of the property is a third party (not the bank), and all proceeds from the sale go to the lender. The lender either forgives the difference or gets a judgement against the borrower requiring them to pay the lender all or part of the difference between the sale price and the original value of the mortgage. In some states this difference must legally be forgiven in a short sale.

Sub S Corp: A corporation that meets specific Internal Revenue Code requirements, giving a corporation with 100 shareholders or less the benefit of incorporation while being taxed as a corporation.

Tax Assessment: The dollar value assigned to a property to measure applicable taxes.

Wholesale Flipping: Real estate wholesaling is similar to flipping except that the time frame is much shorter, and no repairs are made to the home before the wholesaler sells it. A real estate wholesaler contracts with a home seller, markets the home to his potential buyers, and then assigns the contract to the buyer.

APPENDIX

Sample Forms

Financial Statement

Financial Statement

[Name]
[Time Period]

Assets

_____

Net Income

Liabilities

_____

Total Expenses

Net Worth

Repair Costs for Resident Damages

Repair Costs for Resident Damages
BillyEpperhart.com

Resident Name: _____

Property Address: _____

This list is provided at move-in and move-out so you are aware of the cost of property damage, and so you can avoid these expenses. It is understood by the resident that damages resulting from the resident's neglect, abuse, or fault become rent due.

Cleaning (Not done by you):

Refrigerator	$35
Stove top or oven	$25-$50
Kitchen cabinet or countertop	$20
Kitchen or bathroom floor	$30
Bathtub/shower	$25
Toilet	$25
Carpet cleaning or deodorizing	$100-$150
Extensive Cleaning	$75/hour

Damages:

Remove crayon marks	$25
Nail hole repair	$10-$35
Replace interior/exterior door	$150-$250
Replace sliding glass door	$200
Replace faucets	$50
Replace bathroom mirror or cabinet	$50-$75
Replace shower heads	$15
Replace toilet	$175
Replace garbage disposal	$100
Replace countertop	$250-$450
Replace window pane	$75-$150
Replace blinds	$75
Replace tile/linoleum	$300-$450

Repair Costs for Resident Damages (cont.)

Missing Items:

Replace light bulb	$1.50
Light fixture globe	$15
Light fixture	$50
Electrical outlet/switch	$5
Electrical cover plate	$2
Replace key	$2
Replace shower curtain	$10
Replace refrigerator shelf	$25
Replace oven knob	$8
Replace window screen	$25

Additional Charges

Replace door lock	$25
Replace curtain rod or towel bars	$20
Replace smoke detector	$40
Remove junk/debris	$75
Fumigate for fleas	$150
Replace fire extinguisher	$40
Replace thermostat	$75
Remove wallpaper	$150
Repaint wall	$25
Vacuum entire unit	$50
Clear drain stoppage	$75
Fence replacement	$25/foot

Resident agrees that subject to the conditions above, the deposit will be refunded in full within _____ after vacating premises. It is understood that the above amounts are minimum charges.

Resident Name: _____

Resident Signature: _____

Date: _____

Rental Agreement Contract

RENTAL AGREEMENT

1. **PARTIES:** This agreement is entered into on this date_____between the following parties,
   RESIDENT(S):_____and **OWNER / MANAGER:**
   _____. Resident agrees to rent from the owner of the premises
   at the following location subject to the terms and conditions of this agreement.
   RENTAL HOME ADDRESS: _____

2. **MOVE-IN COSTS AMOUNT**

		CHARGE / DESCRIPTION
Rent	$_____	Monthly
Security deposit	$_____	Refundable deposit per agreement
Key deposit	$_____	Refundable deposit per agreement
Additional deposit	$_____	See attached pet addendum
Other	$_____	_____
Total due	$_____	

3. **STANDARD WORRY-FREE PAYMENT METHODS:** Residents may select one of the following Standard Worry Free" payment methods for paying rent during the rental term, so they don't have to worry about late charges every month. Residents agree by signing this agreement to give permission and authorization to arrange for rent collection by the method selected and debit appropriate account(s).

   Preferred Method of Payment Selected:

   _____ Electronic debit from checking account on following days/dates each month: _____
   _____ Electronic debit from savings account on following days/dates each month:_____
   _____ Debit card or credit card debit from following account;_____
   _____ Payroll deduction sent directly from employer biweekly or monthly.

   Payment may be made by traditional methods, such as check or money order, which requires an additional handling fee of $_____per transaction. Please make checks payable to: _____
   Check or money order should be delivered to: _____

4. **EARLY PAYMENT REBATE:** The rent due date is_____The normal rent rate is $_____.
   For rent paid early which is received at least_____days BEFORE the due date, Resident will be entitled to a $_____rebate mailed back to Resident within 10 days after payment is received. Please note, that if Resident is participating in one of the worry-free payment methods and payments are automatically debited early (specified number of days prior to the due date),then the rebate amount is automatically reduced from the total debited.

5. **ON TIME PAYMENT:** Payments made on time for a period of_____months will entitle Resident to choose one free upgrade from the upgrade lists.

6. **LATE PAYMENT CHARGE:** Regular payments are due by the_____. Resident agrees that if rent is not received by 5:00 PM on the due date, Resident shall pay a late payment charge of_____. Any dishonored check shall be treated as unpaid rent, and be subject to a handling fee of $_____,and must be made good by cash, money order, or certified check within 24 hours of notification.

7. **TRADITIONAL DELIVERY OF PAYMENTS:** Please be advised that any payments lost in the mail will be treated as if unpaid until received by Management. If a check is returned unpaid for whatever reason, checks will no longer be accepted for at least six months. Resident will be required to pay by certified funds only. To avoid potential problems, we suggest using one of the worry-free payment methods.

8. **OCCUPANTS:** No more than_____occupants shall occupy the premises, and only the following listed residents; _____

9. **ADDITIONAL RESIDENTS:** Persons other than those specifically listed on the Rental Agreement shall be strictly prohibited from staying in the rental unit for more than 7 consecutive days, or a total of 20 days in any 12-month period. For purposes of this section, "staying in the rental unit" shall include, but not be limited to, long-term or

Rental Agreement Contract (cont.)

regular house guest, live-in babysitters, and visiting relatives. Resident shall notify the Management in writing any time the Resident expects any guest will be staying in excess of the time limits in this paragraph. Additional residents cannot occupy the premised without first being approved by Management and are subject to full screening procedures. If additional residents are accepted, this is also subject to additional rent and security deposit being required. Unauthorized residents are a violation of this agreement and are grounds for termination.

10. **ASSIGNMENT and SUBLETTING:** Resident will not sublet or relet any part of the premises or assign this Agreement without prior consent of the Owner or Management.

11. **UTILITIES:** Resident(s) are responsible for all utility charges, except for the following, which will be paid by Owner:_____.

Our company pays for_____. It is agreed to by Resident that anytime usage of this utility becomes excessive and exceeds_____per month Resident is responsible for payment above this amount and it will be considered additional rent due.

12. **FINANCIAL HARDSHIP:** Because unforeseen circumstances may occur during the rental term which may create difficulty for Resident to make timely rent payment, Resident agrees to work with Owner and permit direct contact from Owner with the following individuals, companies, or organizations for assistance in past-due rental payments. Please provide names and phone numbers of individuals who may be able to provide assistance for payment of rent should you need temporary financial assistance.

Emergency Contact #1
Name: _____   Phone:_____

Emergency Contact #2
Name: _____   Phone:_____

Parent or Cosigner
Name: _____   Phone:_____

Church or nonprofit organization that may be able to assist Resident.
Contact: _____   Phone:_____

Additional agency that may be able to assist Resident.
Contact: _____   Phone: _____

Charge the following credit card # if rent becomes 5 days past due:
_____   Exp. date: _____

Cardholder's signature: _____

13.   **CONDUCT:** Resident family, and guests shall not make or allow unreasonable noise or sound. Resident and/or guests shall not disturb other Residents' peaceful enjoyment of the premises. Disorderly conduct will result in a notice to vacate the premises and termination of agreement. In addition, Residents are responsible for all actions and damages caused by Resident's guests.

14. **NOTICES:** Any notice is deemed served on the day on which it is both mailed by first-class mail to the Resident at the premises, and attached in a secure manner to the main entrance of that portion of the premises of which Resident has possession.

15. **REMEDIES/ATTORNEYS FEES:** Nothing in this Agreement shall limit the right of the Owner to terminate this Agreement as provided by any provision of the Landlord Resident Act. If civil action is instituted in connection with this Agreement, the prevailing party shall be entitled to recover court costs and any reasonable attorneys fees.

16. **MANAGER/AGENT FOR SERVICE:** The name, address, and phone number of the manager and agent for service is:

17. **MAJOR MAINTENANCE GUARANTEE:** Residents understand and agree that the following major repairs are the responsibility of the Owners and Managers:
    1.
    2.
    3.

Rental Agreement Contract (cont.)

The Owners/Managers agree to guarantee that these major repairs will be fixed within 72 hours after notification of the problem to Owner/Manager. Resident understands that if a major repair is not corrected within 72 hours after notification. Resident will receive FREE RENT on a prorated basis starting the fourth day after the day of notification until the problem is corrected. Residents further understand and agree that the 72-hour clock does not start ticking until after the Owner has been directly notified of the problem and provides confirmation of that acknowledgment to Resident. The maintenance guarantee will not be honored if the maintenance problem was caused by the Residents negligence, abuse, or fault. Resident also agrees that in order for the Owner to honor the guarantee, the Owner or Manager must be given access into the building, with Residents permission, to correct the problem. Free rent will be awarded in the form of a cash rebate following the next on-time rent received.

18. **YARD/GROUNDS:** Resident shall properly care for and mow the grass and adequately water the lawn, shrubbery and grounds. If yard is not properly maintained, Management reserves the right to hire someone to mow or care for yard and charge the expense to Resident as additional rent after first advising Resident that they have 72 hours to handle the responsibility. In regard to yard upkeep, Manager is only responsible for _____

19. **ABANDONMENT:** Any goods, vehicles, or other property left on the premise after termination of the tenancy by any means shall be considered abandoned and disposed of as provided by statute.

20. **COMPLIANCE WITH THE LAW:** Resident shall not violate any applicable local, state, or federal law or regulation in or about the premises.

21. **INSURANCE:** Owner and Management are not responsible for any loss or damage to property owned by Resident or guests unless resulting from Managements intentional or negligent acts. It is understood that all residents should carry renter's insurance for fire, extended coverage, and liability to cover accidental injury and damage or loss of personal property due to fire or theft.

22. **NONWAIVER AND ACCEPTING PAYMENTS:** Should the Owner or Manager accept any partial or late rent payments, this in no way constitutes a waiver of the Owner, nor affects any notice of eviction proceedings previously given. Waiver by either party of strict performance of any provision of this agreement shall not be a waiver of or prejudice the party's right to require strict performance of the same provision in the future or any other provision.

23. **PETS:** Resident and/or guests shall not maintain any pets upon the premises, without prior written consent of Management. No animal, bird, or fish of any kind will be kept on the premises, even temporarily, except properly trained dogs needed by blind, deaf, or disabled persons and only under the following circumstances _____ _____. If a pet is accepted (not referring to trained dogs for assistance), this is subject to payment of a higher monthly rent and additional deposit. Please refer to Pet Addendum (if applicable).

24. **EXTENDED ABSENCE:** Resident will notify Landlord in advance if Resident will be away from the premises for _____ or more consecutive days. During such absence, Landlord may enter the premises at times reasonably necessary to maintain the property and inspect for needed repairs.

25. **DISCLOSURES:** Resident acknowledges that Landlord has made the following disclosures:

    _____   Disclosure of information on Lead-Based Paint and/or Lead-Based Paint Hazards

    _____   Other disclosure: _____

26. **FUTURE HOMEBUYER:** Residents understand and agree that, following each on-time payment received, the Owner has agreed to increase the amount of money by $_____ the Resident will be entitled to receive toward purchase of a home at time of closing. The total amount will be referred to as the Future Homebuyers Account for the Resident during the term of the rental. Residents will be able to receive a credit at closing equal to the amount in their Future Homebuyers Account once they have been a resident for a minimum of _____ years. Money equivalent to the Future Homebuyers Account is to be used solely for the purchase of a house and is credited or paid out at time of real estate closing. The house Resident may purchase and apply the Future Homebuyers Account towards can be selected from either the same residence in this agreement or a home offered from one of the following builders or brokers:_____.

Please note that the money total increases each month with every on-time payment received by the following due date:_____. If, however, payment is received late, the total money accrued into the Homebuyers Account

Rental Agreement Contract (cont.)

up to that point becomes null and void. The account starts again to accumulate with the next on-time rental payment. Residents further understand and agree that Residents are:

- Responsible for handling all minor repairs, subject to Resident paying the first $100 of any repair, unless the repair is needed because of the negligence of the Owner or Manager. In that case Owner is responsible for the total cost of the repair.
- To pass semiannual property inspections.
- To annually attend a maintenance class or training offered to residents.

By meeting those three requirements, Residents will receive an additional $_____ every 6 months (following each inspection) added toward their Future Homebuyers Account. Two property inspections are conducted yearly with a checklist provided to Residents in advance of inspections. Failure to handle minor repairs or failure to pass a property inspection nullifies the total amount accumulated up to that point in the Resident's Future Homebuyers Account.

27. **SATISFACTORY INSPECTION:** Resident has personally inspected the premises, and finds it satisfactory at the time of execution of this agreement, except as noted on the Property Condition Checklist.

28. **NO OTHER PROMISES:** No promises have been made to Resident except as contained in this Agreement, and as follows:

29. **USE OF PREMISES:** The premises shall be used as a dwelling unit and for no other purposes. Resident shall use, in a reasonable manner, all facilities, utilities, and appliances on the premises and shall maintain the premises and facilities in a clean and sanitary condition at all times, and upon termination of the tenancy shall surrender the premises in as good condition as when received, ordinary wear and tear and damage by the elements excepted. Resident further agrees to make all utility payments (that are listed in their name) on time during the term of this tenancy and will be considered in breach of this Agreement for nonpayment and will be held liable for any resulting added charges and damages.

30. **PLUMBING:** Expense or damage caused by stoppage of waste pipes or overflow of bathtubs, toilets, or wash-basins caused by Residents conduct shall be Residents responsibility.

31. **ALTERATIONS:** Resident shall not tamper with or make alterations (including painting, nail holes, contact, or wallpaper) to the premises without Manager's prior written consent. All curtains, mini-blinds, fixtures, shelves, and carpet present in the premises before move-in, must remain when resident vacates. In addition, locks may not be changed or added without Owner's or Manager's prior written permission. And if permission is granted, a copy of ally new keys will be given to the management within three days after the change. If Resident is locked out of tile premises, there is a charge of $ to open the premises between the hours of and a charge of $ for opening the premises beyond those hours. Additional charges apply if a key is lost and locks must be changed.

32. **VEHICLES:** Only authorized vehicles may be parked on the premises. These vehicles include:
All vehicles kept on the premises must be operational and have current registration, tags, decals, and license required by local and state laws. Any vehicle not meeting these requirements or unauthorized vehicles will be removed at Resident's expense after being given 72-hour notification. Vehicles must be parked only on paved or designated areas. Resident further understands that no repairing, servicing, or painting of the vehicle is permitted on the premises. Resident also agrees never to park or store a recreational vehicle, motor home, or trailer of any type.

Rental Agreement Contract (cont.)

33. **REPAIRS/REPORTING:** Resident shall notify Manager immediately in writing of all equipment malfunctions, failure to supply services, or repairs needed. Resident shall not tamper with or repair heating/AC or locks without first obtaining written consent of owner. If need for repair is due to Resident's fault, neglect, or abuse repair costs become rent that is due. (Resident agrees to pay for repairs within_____days. If payment is not made in the specified time the amount due will be deducted from the rental deposit and a charge of % per annum will accrue?).

34. **INDEMNIFICATION:** Resident shall indemnify and hold owner harmless from any claim, loss, or liability arising out of or related to any activity on premises of Resident and any guest. Residents duty to indemnify shall not apply to or prevent any claim by Resident against Manager for injury or damage to Resident or Residents property for which Manager may be liable.

35. **FREE UPGRADE REFERRAL:** The owner agrees to offer a free property upgrade once a year to any Resident who recommends and refers just one qualified prospective resident to one of our rentals during the course of any year. In order for current residents to qualify for the free property upgrade, any referred prospective resident must:

    - Fill out a rental application
    - Meet the minimum resident criteria
    - Either move-in to one of Owner's rentals (paying all required funds) or pay $100 fee to be placed on the Owners priority waiting list, which is refundable if Owner does not find housing that matches stated preferences of referred future Resident within a 90 day period.

36. **SECURITY DEPOSIT:** The sum set forth on this Rental Agreement has been deposited with Manager upon execution of this agreement as a security deposit to be applied to remedy any default by Resident in performance of Residents obligations under the lease and to repair damages to the premises caused by Resident, not including ordinary wear and tear. Within_____days after termination of the lease and delivery of possession of the leased premises to Manager, Manager shall refund the deposit or shall give Resident an accounting of Manager's claim to the deposit. If costs or repairing damages exceed the amount of the deposit Resident shall be responsible for all such excess costs. Resident may not at any time apply the security deposit to be used as last months rent or any other sum due under this Agreement.

37. **APPLIANCES:** Unless otherwise stated as part of the custom rental package, this Rental Agreement does NOT include any appliances. Appliances that are located on the premises are there solely at the convenience of the Owner, who assumes no responsibility for their operation. While on the premises, Residents are free to use them; however, Residents do so at their own risk. In the event appliances fail to function, Owner is not liable for repair or damages. If Residents wish, at anytime they may request that the appliances be removed. Owner will dispose of them at his/her expense.

38. **MANAGER'S RIGHT TO ACCESS:** Manager shall have the right to enter the premises in order to inspect the premises, make necessary or agreed repairs or improvements, supply necessary or agreed services, or show the premises to prospective residents, purchasers, or contractors. Except in case of emergency, agreement to the contrary by Resident or unless it is impractical to do so, Manager shall give Resident at least 24 hours notice of Manager's intent to enter and may enter only at reasonable times. Manager shall also have the right to enter the premises when Resident has abandoned or surrendered the premises, or during any absence of Resident in excess of 7 days. Resident shall not unreasonably withhold consent for Manager to enter the premises.

39. **RESIDENT'S TERMINATION NOTICE:** Resident may not terminate this Rental Agreement without 30-days written notice if this is a month-to-month tenancy. Failure of Resident to provide appropriate written notice to terminate a month-to-month tenancy will result in a Resident's continuing obligation under this Agreement for up to thirty (30) days.

40. **LIENS:** Except with respect to activities for which Manager is responsible, Resident shall pay as due all claims for work done on and for services rendered or material furnished to the premises, and shall keep the premises free from any liens caused by Resident's failure to meet Resident's obligations.

41. **DAMAGE AND DESTRUCTION:** In the event the premises are severely damaged or destroyed by fire or other casualty, either party may terminate the lease. In the event damage was caused by Resident's action or neglect, Resident will be held liable for all damages.

42. **BUILD YOUR CREDIT REPUTATION:** A review of each Resident's performance is performed every six months and Owner will provide residents with a copy of a GOOD performance report when so earned. Good reports are earned by Residents who pay on time and follow ALL terms of the Rental Agreement. Residents can then give copies of their report to future landlords, loan officers, banks, and mortgage companies. These reports may be

Rental Agreement Contract (cont.)

beneficial in helping you rent or buy a car or house in the future. Building your credit reputation may also help Residents participating in the Future Homebuyers Program. Please note: a poor payment performance and any judgments are reported to national credit agencies and will be made available to future landlords, banks, and other creditors that residents may want to do business with in the future. Therefore, it is important that Residents understand that the credit they establish with Owner and the reputation they develop through performance reports during the rental term (good or bad) can follow Residents for many years. Because of such importance of performances reported, Resident will always be notified when a nonpayment or rental violation occurs and Resident will be given an opportunity to immediately correct any poor performance before it is reported.

43. **JOINT LIABILITY:** Each person signing this Agreement as a Resident is jointly and severally liable for all the terms of this agreement.

44. **ADDITIONAL PROVISIONS AND MODIFICATIONS TO THIS:** Any additions or modifications to this Agreement must be in writing. The following additional provisions are part of this agreement:

45. **VALIDITY OF EACH PART:** If any portion of this Agreement is held to be invalid, its invalidity will not affect the enforceability of any other provision.

46. **GROUNDS FOR TERMINATION**: The failure of Resident or guests to comply with any term of this Agreement is grounds for termination, with appropriate notice and procedures required by law.

47. **READ THIS ENTIRE AGREEMENT:** Resident has read all the stipulations contained in the Rental Agreement agrees to comply, and has received a copy thereof.

Residents signature:_____Date_____

Residents signature:_____Date_____

Owner/Manager/Agent signature:_____Date _____

Recommended Reading

The ABC's of Real Estate Investing: The Secrets of Finding Hidden Profits Most Investors Miss **by Ken McElroy**

Real Estate Riches: How to Become Rich Using Your Banker's Money **by Dolf De Roos, Ph.D.**

Real Estate Loop-Holes: Secrets of Successful Real Estate Investing **by Diane Kennedy, C.P.A. and Garrett Sutton, Esq.**

Successful Real Estate Investing: How to Avoid the 75 Most Costly Mistakes Every Investor Makes **by Robert Shemin**

The Beginner's Guide to Real Estate Investing **by Gary W. Eldred, Ph.D.**

How to be a Quick Turn Real Estate Millionaire: Make Fast Cash with No Money, Credit, or Previous Experience **by Ron LeGrand**

The Complete Idiot's Guide to Making Money with Rental Properties **by Brian F. Edwards, Casey Edwards, and Susannah Craig-Edwards**

How to Rent Vacation Properties by Owner: The Complete Guide to Buy, Manage, Furnish, Rent, Maintain and Advertise your Vacation Rental Investment **by Christine Hrib Karpinski**

Successful Real Estate Investing in a Boom or Bust Market **by Larry B. Loftis, Esq.**

The Real Estate Fast Track: How to Create a $5,000 to $50,000 per Month Real Estate Cash Flow **by David Finkel**

Entrepreneur's Great Big Book on Real Estate Investing: Everything You Need to Know to Create Wealth in Real Estate **by Stuart Leland Rider**

Real Estate for Boomers and Beyond: Exploring the Costs, Choices and Changes for Your Next Move **by Tom Kelly**

Buy and Hold: 7 Steps to a Real Estate Fortune **by David Schumacher, Ph.D.**

Bubbles, Booms and Busts: Make Money in Any Real Estate Market **by Blanche Evans**

From 0 to 130 Properties in 3.5 Years **by Steve McKnight**

Tips and Traps When Mortgage Hunting **by Robert Irwin**

Be a Real Estate Millionaire: Secrets Strategies for Lifetime Wealth Today **by Dean Graziosi**

The Coming Crash in the Housing Market: 10 Things You Can Do Now to Protect Your Most Valuable Investment **by John R. Talbott**

Insider Secrets to Financing Your Real Estate Investments: What Every Real Estate Investor Needs to Know About Finding and Financing Your Next Deal **by Frank Gallinelli**

What Every Real Estate Investor Needs to Know About Cash Flow… And 36 Other Key Financial Measures **by Frank Gallinelli**

Investing in Real Estate, Third Edition **by Andrew McLean and Gary W. Eldred, Ph.D.**

The Weekend Millionaire's Secrets to Investing in Real Estate **by Mike Summey and Roger Dawson**

Real Estate Investing from A to Z: The Most Comprehensive, Practical, and Readable Guide to Investing Profitably in Real Estate, Third Edition **by William H. Pivar**

Getting Started in Real Estate Investing, **by Second Edition Michael C. Thomsett and Jean Freestone Thomsett**

What No One Ever Tells You About Investing in Real Estate: Real-Life Advice from 101 Successful Investors **by Robert J. Hill II, Esq.**

All Real Estate Is Local: What You Need to Know to Profit in Real Estate—In a Buyer's and a Seller's Market **by David Lereah**

Trump Strategies for Real Estate: Billionaire Lessons for the Small Investor **by George H. Ross with Andrew James McLean**

Investing in Duplexes, Triplexes and Quads: The Fastest and Safest Way to Real Estate Wealth **by Larry B. Loftis, Esq.**

Buy, Rent and Sell: How to Profit by Investing in Residential Real Estate **by Robert Irwin**

Start Small, Profit Big in Real Estate: Fixer Jay's 2-Year Plan for Building Wealth—Starting from Scratch! **by Jay P. DeCima**

The Landlord's Kit: A Complete Set of Ready-to-Use Forms, Letters, and Notices to Increase Profits, Take Control, and Eliminate the Hassles of Property Management **by Jeffrey Taylor**

The Millionaire Real Estate Investor **by Gary Keller with Dave Jenks and Jay Papasan**

Flipping Properties: Generate Instant Cash Profits in Real Estate **by William Bronchick and Robert Dahlstrom**

Value Investing in Real Estate **by Gary W. Eldred, Ph.D.**

The Unofficial Guide to Real Estate Investing **by Martin Stone and Spencer Strauss**

Real Estate Debt Can Make You Rich: What You Owe Today Is What You Will Be Worth Tomorrow **by Steve Dexter**

Timing the Real Estate Market **by Craig Hall**

The Insider's Guide to Making Money in Real Estate: Smart Steps to Building Your Wealth through Property **by Dolf De Roos, Ph.D. and Diane Kennedy, CPA**

Maverick Real Estate Investing: The Art of Buying and Selling Properties like Trump, Zell, Simon, and the World's Greatest Land Owners **by Steve Bergsman**

The Smart Money Guide to Real Estate Investing **by Gerri Willis**

Nothing Down: A Proven Program That Shows You How to Buy Real Estate with Little or No Money Down **by Robert G. Allen**

Streetwise Investing in Rental Housing: A Detailed Strategy for Financial Independence **by H. Roger Neal**

All About Real Estate Investing: The Easy Way to Get Started, Second Edition **by William Benke and Joseph M. Fowler**

Investing in a Vacation Home for Pleasure and Profit **by James H. Boykin**

Unlimited Riches: Making Your Fortune in Real Estate Investing **by Robert Shemin**

How to Get Started in Real Estate Investing **by Robert Irwin**

How to Find Hidden Real Estate Bargains: For Home Buyers and Investors Looking to Uncover a Wealth of Opportunities **by Robert Irwin**

5 Magic Paths to Making a Fortune in Real Estate: Learn How to Buy, Renovate, and Sell **by James Lumley**

The Real Estate Millionaire: How to Invest in Rental Markets and Make a Fortune **by Boaz Gilad and Susanne Gilad**

Make More Money Investing in Multi-units: A Step-by-Step Guide to Profiting from Apartment Buildings **by Gregory D. Warr**

How to Make $1,000,000 in Real Estate in Three Years Starting With No Cash **by Tyler G. Hicks**

Rich Dad's Real Estate Advantages: Tax and Legal Secrets of Successful Real Estate Investors **by Sharon L. Lechter and Garrett Sutton Esq.**

How to Make Big Money in Real Estate **by Tyler G. Hicks**

How to Buy and Sell Apartment Buildings **by Eugene E. Vollucci**

The Complete Guide to Buying and Selling Apartment Buildings **by Steve Berges**

Make Millions by Buying Small Apartment Properties in Your Spare Time **by Brian K. Friedman**

How a Second Home Can Be Your Best Investment **by Tom Kelly and John Tuccillo**

Building Wealth One House at a Time **by John W. Schaub**

2 Years to a Million in Real Estate **by Matthew A. Martinez**

Building Wealth: From Rags to Riches through Real Estate **by Russ Whitney**

Unlimited Real Estate Profit: Create Wealth and Build a Financial Fortress through Today's Real Estate Investing **by Mark Stephan Garrison, M.B.A. and Paula Tripp-Garrison**

Are You Missing the Real Estate Boom? Why Home Values and Other Real Estate Investments Will Climb through the End of the Decade—and How to Profit From Them **by David Lereah**

Successful Real Estate Investing, a Practical Guide to Profits for the Small Investor **by Peter G. Miller**

Getting Started in Rental Income **by Michael C. Thomsett**

Secrets of a Millionaire Real Estate Investor **by Robert Shemin, Esq.**

ABOUT THE AUTHOR

AUTHOR BILLY EPPERHART received his M.B.A. from Colorado State University. Describing himself as a serial entrepreneur, Billy has started seven businesses and owned two franchises. As a real estate investor, he simultaneously owned investment properties in five different states.

Currently, Billy directs two nonprofit companies and is co-director of the Business School of Charis Bible College and serves on the board of Andrew Wommack Ministries. He and his wife, Becky, make their home in Colorado. For more information or to enjoy his weekly financial blog, visit www.billyepperhart.com.

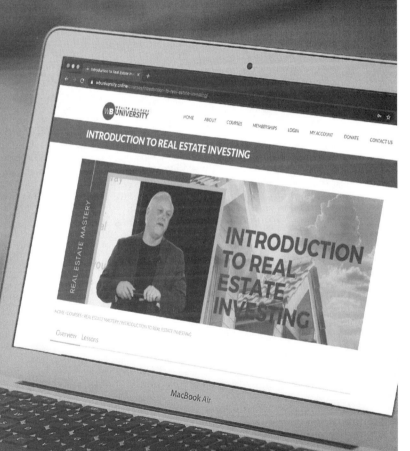

The Harrison House Vision

Proclaiming the truth and the power

of the Gospel of Jesus Christ with excellence.

Challenging Christians

to live victoriously,

grow spiritually,

know God intimately.

Connect with us on

f Facebook @ HarrisonHousePublishers

and ⓘ Instagram @ HarrisonHousePublishing

so you can stay up to date with news

about our books and our authors.

Visit us at **www.harrisonhouse.com**

for a complete product listing as well as

monthly specials for wholesale distribution.